TWAYNE'S WORLD AUTHORS SERIES

A *Survey of the World's Literature*

Sylvia E. Bowman, Indiana University

GENERAL EDITOR

FRANCE

Maxwell A. Smith, Guerry Professor of French, Emeritus
The University of Chattanooga
Former Visiting Professor in Modern Languages
The Florida State University

EDITOR

Leconte de Lisle

(TWAS 278)

TWAYNE'S WORLD AUTHORS SERIES (TWAS)

The purpose of TWAS is to survey the major writers—novelists, dramatists, historians, poets, philosophers, and critics—of the nations of the world. Among the national literatures covered are those of Australia, Canada, China, Eastern Europe, France, Germany, Greece, Italy, Japan, Latin America, the Netherlands, New Zealand, Poland, Russia, Scandinavia, Spain, and the African nations, as well as Hebrew, Yiddish, and Latin Classical literature. This survey is complemented by Twayne's United States Authors Series and English Authors Series.

The intent of each volume in these series is to present a critical-analytical study of the works of the writer; to include biographical and historical material that may be necessary for understanding, appreciation, and critical appraisal of the writer; and to present all material in clear, concise English—but not to vitiate the scholarly content of the work by doing so.

Leconte de Lisle

By ROBERT T. DENOMMÉ

University of Virginia

Twayne Publishers, Inc. :: New York

Library of Congress Catalog Card Number: 73-1844

ISBN 0–8057–2518–0

MANUFACTURED IN THE UNITED STATES OF AMERICA

To
JEAN-ALBERT BÉDÉ
MASTER TEACHER AND SCHOLAR

Preface

This study of the critical and poetical works of Leconte de Lisle
is aimed at the general reader whose lack of any first-hand ac-
quaintance with the French language may have discouraged him
from a systematic reading of the verse of this distinguished Parnassian poet. To make these essays on the life and work of
Leconte de Lisle accessible to those who possess no prior knowledge of the intricacies of French versification, I have made every
attempt to keep the purely technical considerations to an absolute
minimum. Only those facts which directly or indirectly have a
bearing on the critical and poetical attitudes of de Lisle have been
included in the brief biographical account which precedes the
chapters that examine the poet's aesthetic code. There are separate chapters which survey and analyze Leconte de Lisle's principal collections, the *Poèmes antiques,* the *Poèmes barbares,* the
Poèmes tragiques and the *Derniers Poèmes.* I have made prose
approximations in English of all the verse which is cited in order
to illustrate the various points that are made. Likewise, I have
translated into English all of the theoretical and critical excerpts
which are quoted. Because the verse of Leconte de Lisle is not
readily available today in Anglo-Saxon countries, the original
poetry that is translated in the text has been retained in the notes
at the end of the study.

My ambition has been to present as comprehensive a view of
Leconte de Lisle as possible without resorting to too many details
and allusions which might detract from such an objective. Consequently, Leconte de Lisle's youthful prose and poetry are invoked
only insofar as they shed light on the dominant attitudes which
inform his published work. Emphasis has been placed on those
works which are associated with his so-called Parnassian period.

Preface

It is a pleasure for me to record my gratitude to the University of Virginia which granted me a Sesquicentennial Fellowship to complete this study.

ROBERT T. DENOMMÉ

Charlottesville, Virginia

Contents

Chronology

1818   October 22: Charles-René Marie Leconte de Lisle born on the island of Réunion (formerly Bourbon) off the southeast coast of Africa.

1822   Leaves Réunion with his parents for Nantes, France.

1828   Returns to island. Attends school at the Collège de Saint-Denis.

1837   Sent to Dinan to live with an uncle, Louis Leconte, the deputy mayor of the Breton city. Enrolls in the Law School of the University of Rennes, but is ostensibly more interested in attending lectures in history and literature in the Faculty of Letters.

1839   Collaborates with a friend, Julien Rouffet, on a collection of poems, "Le Coeur et l'Ame," which remains unpublished.

1840   Founder and editor of the literary journal, *La Variété*, which folds after eleven months.

1842   Begins the satirical review, *Le Scorpion*, which also fails within a year for lack of sufficient funds.

1843   Returns to Réunion without the law degree his parents had expected him to earn. His allowance cut off, he must perform menial tasks for several business concerns in order to subsist. Increasing disenchantment with his family and the creoles of Réunion.

1845   Leaves Réunion for France. Member of the staff for the Fourierist daily newspaper, *La Démocratie pacifique*. He is subsequently appointed secretary and editor of the companion review, *La Phalange*, to which he contributes poems and short stories.

1846   Meets and befriends the noted Hellenist, Louis Ménard, the translator, Thalès Bernard, and the poet, Pierre Dubois.

1848   An ardent republican, he is sent to Dinan, a stronghold of conservatism, to argue the liberal cause. He openly advocates the abolition of slavery which further strains his relationship with his family in Réunion.

1849 Disassociates himself from *La Démocratie pacifique* and *La Phalange*. His application for a teaching position at the Collège de Saint-Denis is rejected by the government administration of Réunion.

1850 Disheartened by the failure of the revolution, he turns away from politics. Becomes enamored of Marie Jobbé-Duval, the wife of his close friend, the artist Félix Jobbé-Duval.

1852 Publication of the *Poèmes antiques*.

1853 Granted a small pension by the Administrative Council of Réunion.

1855 Publication of *Poèmes et poésies*.

1857 Gains a measure of public recognition when the French Academy awards him the Lambert Prize for his collection, *Poèmes et poésies*. Marries Anne Adélaide Perray at Saint-Sulpice.

1861 Publication of his translation of Theocritus' *Odes* and *Idylls*.

1862 Publication of the *Poésies barbares*, subsequently called the *Poèmes barbares*.

1864 Young poets interested in the renovation of poetry are invited to meet with Leconte de Lisle and his young wife in their apartment on the Boulevard des Invalides on Saturday evenings. Accepts an annual pension of 3,600 francs from Louis-Napoleon's private budget.

1866 Alphonse Lemerre publishes the eighteen installments which will comprise the first volume of the *Parnasse contemporain*. The second number is comprised entirely of Leconte de Lisle's verse. Publication of his translation of Homer's *Iliad*.

1867 Publication of his translation of *The Odyssey*.

1868 A cyclone devastates Réunion; for economic reasons, the Islanders are compelled to eliminate his pension.

1869 Leconte de Lisle is widely acknowledged as head of the Parnassian school or movement.

1870 Publication of the pamphlet, *Le Catéchisme populaire républicain*.

1871 Appearance of two more pamphlets, *Histoire populaire de la Révolution française* and *Histoire populaire du Christianisme*. Publication of the second volume of the *Parnasse contemporain*, delayed two years by the Franco-Prussian War.

1872 The *Poèmes et poésies* of 1855 are transferred to augmented edition of the *Poèmes antiques* and *Poèmes barbares*.

1873 His translation of Aeschylus' tragedy, *Les Erinnyes*, is mounted for presentation at the Odéon with incidental music composed by Massenet. Accepts an assistant librarianship at the Senate and a stipend of 2,700 francs annually.

1876 Contributes poems to the third volume of the *Parnasse contemporain*.

1884 Publication of the *Poèmes tragiques*. Decorated as Officier de la Légion d'Honneur by Jules Ferry.

1886 Elected a member of the Académie Française, succeeding Victor Hugo.

1894 July 17: Death of Leconte de Lisle resulting from an attack of influenza. July 21: Funeral in the church of Saint-Sulpice.

1895 Publication of the *Derniers Poèmes*, edited by J. M. de Heredia.

CHAPTER 1

The Life of a Poet

THE alternating voices of optimism and pessimism discernible in Leconte de Lisle's aesthetic theory and poetic practice betray the agonized predicament of a man whose personal aspiration ran counter to an interpretation of reality fashioned by a society bent on reaping the practical advantages of applied science and industrialism. From his earliest years as an adolescent on the island of Réunion to his maturity as a journalist and a poet in France, Leconte de Lisle lived in spiritual exile from a nation which sought so resolutely to pay homage to the burgeoning forces of nineteenth-century materialism. To a significant extent, the disenchantment he experienced resulted from a compelling need to find corroboration for an instinctive longing for permanence in a world singularly bereft of such permanence. Leconte de Lisle's most successful verse bespeaks the tragedy of a poet who sought relentlessly to achieve a measure of harmony between the spiritual and material aspects of existence. Most of his verse attempts something considerably more than to describe the physical and concrete world of the past in aesthetically pleasing language. If his scrupulous attention to form and detail endows his work with an unusual degree of explicitness, his near-obsessive preoccupation with sensuous beauty and perfection invests, at moments, his lyricism with allusive references and intimations that wing beyond the recognizable world of appearances. His pessimism proceeded from the new scientific and intellectual attitudes which forced him to put his idealism to a severe and all but impossible test. His optimism sprang from a marked determination to supplement the inadequacy of an unsatisfying reality by the creation of lasting works of art which might survive great civilizations. Leconte de Lisle's lyricism was crucially informed by the times in which he lived. The account of his response to the events which shaped nineteenth-century France is also the account of the genesis of his poetry.

I *The Early Years*

The brilliant evocations of exotic luxuriance and the expressions of nostalgic longing which punctuate Leconte de Lisle's verse in such lyrically superb instances as "La Fontaine aux lianes" and "Le Manchy" doubtless spring from the reassuring recollection of a happy childhood. The eldest of six children, Charles-Marie René, the future poet, was born at Saint-Paul de la Réunion on October 22, 1818. His father, a former surgeon's aide in Napoleon's army, had emigrated some years earlier to the small tropical island off the southeast coast of Africa during the Bourbon Restoration, married a young creole of aristocratic lineage,[1] and settled on a plantation to raise sugar cane. Except for the period between his third and tenth years which were spent in Nantes, France, Leconte de Lisle led a relatively pleasant and carefree existence in the lush surroundings of the tropical island. His cultured parents took charge of his early schooling, tutoring him in such eighteenth-century *philosophes* as Voltaire and Rousseau and encouraging the development of a kind of Deism and anticlericalism which made him distrustful of the claims of Christianity at a very precocious age.

At the nearby Collège de Saint-Denis where more formal instruction was provided until his departure for Brittany in 1837, Leconte de Lisle immersed himself in the verse of Millevoye and Parny, poets very much in vogue during that time, and in the earliest works of Lamartine, Victor Hugo, and Walter Scott. The dozen or so poems composed and carefully copied out on the ruled pages of his college theme books divulge the influence and inspiration of Lamartine's *Méditations poétiques*. If his readings in the abbé Guillaume Raynal awakened his curiosity about the history of primitive peoples, the fictional recreations of Walter Scott excited at once his imagination and poetic sensibility. He grew fond of memorizing the various *Fables of La Fontaine*,[2] but the greatest impression made on the budding poet during these years remained unquestionably Victor Hugo. His reading of the *Orientales* constituted a veritable revelation to Leconte de Lisle, the experience of which he chose to relay publicly in his acceptance discourse to the French Academy many years later:

As far as I am concerned, I am still unable to recall without feeling deeply indebted for the great shock I experienced when, as a youth, I was handed this volume [*Les Orientales*] as I sat in the mountains of my native island. As I read it, I experienced a vision of a world enshrined completely in light, and I admired the wealth of such new and daring images, conveyed in a wave of irresistible lyricism and expressed in language which was as precise as it was sonorous. It was, to me, as if an immense light had suddenly illuminated the sea, the mountains, the forests, the entire landscape of my country whose beauty and unusual charm, up to that time, I had never truly perceived except only in the confused and unconscious manner of a child.[3]

Given his background at home and at school during the 1820's and 1830's, it would have been understandable if Leconte de Lisle had elected to cast his lot with the effusive Romantic poets who so readily managed to find their way into print. There is little reason to believe that the future poet ever evinced any real concern for the problems which complicated the lives of the inhabitants of Réunion while he was a schoolboy. Rather, the rich and natural sonorities which emanated from the sea, the forests, and the mountains of the tropical island encouraged the carefree and dreamy disposition of the young man more than they instilled in him any truly sustained awareness of the sordid problems associated with everyday survival.

If it remains true that Leconte de Lisle never experienced as a youth the kind of exaltation usually identified with amorous passion, the presence of his lovely creole cousin, Elixenne de Lanux, at Saint-Paul did elicit his discreet if not platonic admiration. His celebration, many years later, of the memory of Elixenne in such poems as "Le Manchy" and "Le Frais Matin," for example, strikes us as much less the exalted expression of love verse than the crystallization of an experience idealized retrospectively. Indeed, Leconte de Lisle's reaction to his beautiful cousin emerges as one of the earliest clues to the real disposition of the budding poet. To a very important extent, Leconte de Lisle's subsequent lyrical production will underscore the problem of purifying the present by systematic reference to the past, of fashioning the ideal from the real by increasing identification with a remote era. This conflict between reality and idealism, never really satisfactorily resolved in his poetry, very likely asserted itself in Leconte de Lisle's mind as he silently observed at a distance Elixenne de Lanux being brought to Sunday church services in a *manchy* (palanquin) carried by slaves.

II *Apprenticeship and Aspiration*

If the young Leconte de Lisle's departure from his native island in 1837 marked the end of a quasi-idyllic existence, his arrival in Brittany ushered in a period of a growing social and metaphysical awareness which was destined to leave an indelible impression on the mind of the aspiring poet. The dramatic contrast provided by the sunlit tropical Réunion he had left and the bleak and forbidding terrain of the Breton province he encountered was sufficient to produce feelings of disorientation and dissatisfaction within him. Clearly, the more complicated world he was now obliged to face and to dominate issued him a greater and less inviting challenge than had the southeastern African land of his childhood and adolescence. His parents had sent him to Brittany and entrusted him to the care of an uncle, Louis Leconte, the deputy mayor of Dinan, so that he might complete his baccalaureat studies and enter the Law School of the University of Rennes. Charles-Marie René, it will be recalled, was the eldest of six children, and his parents were understandably concerned that he enter a profession which would make him financially independent. But the law career they had chosen for their son held little appeal for him. For the first significant time in his life, the young Leconte de Lisle became conscious of a conflict of desire which separated him from his parents. The manner in which he was to choose to resolve the conflict would give new direction to his life.

After successfully completing the requirements for his baccalaureat diploma in October of 1938 with distinction in French,[4] Leconte de Lisle registered for law studies at the University of Rennes. What captured his real interest, however, were the courses and lectures offered in the Humanities division of the university. Indeed, he neglected his law classes and studies to such an extent that he was barred from taking the first-year examinations. Yet, from the perspective of his subsequent career as a leading Parnassian poet, the academic year spent at Rennes proved to be as enriching as it was stimulating. The lectures which he attended on biblical poetry, Greek and Latin tragedy, primitive literature and mythology provided important background information for

[16]

shaping many later poems which found their way into such collections as the *Poèmes antiques* and the *Poèmes barbares.*[5]

The virtual state of penury to which he was reduced during his his student days at Rennes induced him to reflect upon the composition of a society which struck him as essentially mercantile and harsh in its materialism. His dormant aversion for organized religion, inherited through his earlier readings in the French *philosophes,* reawakened in increasing intensity as he observed the narrowly bigoted behavior of the fervently religious inhabitants of Dinan and Rennes. Feeling more and more removed from the mainstream of society, he read widely in the poetic works of Byron, Vigny and Auguste Barbier, and concluded that he also wished to register the sense of frustration he felt in verse. With Julien Rouffet, a clerk whom he had previously befriended, he composed a series of poetic meditations entitled, "Le Coeur et l'Ame." Although the poems never found their way into print, the two budding poets continued to exchange correspondence in which they voiced disgust over the dubious values adopted by society. De Lisle's letter to Rouffet dated January, 1839, underscores to what point he had grown disenchanted with the age in which he was expected to function: "It is truly a sad example of the egoism of our age; of an age in which the perjury of politics is allowed, without impunity, to contribute to a moral degradation, so grotesquely covered up by a veil of wretched prudery and religious affectation; of an age which only acknowledges gold as its God and which tramples down anyone who worships truth and beauty. For shame!" [6]

Leconte de Lisle's founding of the monthly review, *La Variété,* with Charles Bénézit in Rennes in 1840, constituted a vigorous attempt to combat the major attitudes of a society which kept him midway between hope and exasperation. Somewhat vaguely organized around the motifs of charity and fraternity, the journal saw but eleven issues before it was forced to fold for lack of substantial numbers of subscribers and poor financial backing. The articles which de Lisle contributed to *La Variété* shed considerable light on the elaboration of the philosophy which would loom so importantly behind his later poetical works. Already discernible in his essays was the identification he made between poetry and religion in the sense that true lyricism was the spontaneous expression of the soul and not merely the expression of an individual's feelings or sentiments. One of the major themes which de Lisle was to develop in the *Poèmes antiques* and the *Poèmes barbares* centered precisely about the notion that ideal beauty, energy, and spontaneity were alien to the modern age of Industrialism and Utility.[7] Wavering somewhat between an outwearing allegiance to Lamartine and genuine admiration for André Chénier, de Lisle paid handsome tribute to the two poets who contributed most significantly to the rediscovery and the regeneration of the sources of true lyricism. Many of the pronouncements contained in the article, "André Chénier: de la poésie lyrique à la fin du XVIIIe siècle" (August, 1840), as a matter of fact, strike us as remarkably identical with some of the major critical principles advanced decades later in the prefaces to his best-known collections of verse. If any single *idée force,* may be said to underscore the three essays which de Lisle contributed to *La Variété* as its editor, it is certainly the notion that the unlikely coupling of such writers as Hoffmann, Sheridan, and Chénier sought in their respective manners to rescue literary expression from the decadence and degeneracy into which it had fallen since the early seventeenth century. But if the young editor voiced his reaction against corruptive influences of an exaggerated Romantic sentimentality, he refrained most conspicuously from advocating a psychological and artistic return to the spirit of Ancient Greece. His enthusiasm for André Chénier, especially, is deliberately tempered to satisfy the obvious expectations of readers who held to Christian orientations in art and literature: "André Chénier was a pagan in his thoughts, recollections and inspiration, but he was also the regenerator and monarch of real lyrical form and expression. Another great mind, possessing the same sense and feeling for harmony, succeeded him, to the great glory of our nation! This gentle and religious genius revealed to us a spiritualized Chénier, a disciple and follower of Christ. This sublime liberator who was as great as Chénier because of his sentiments and his concern for form, was M. de Lamartine!" [8]

What emerges clearly from his sojourn in Brittany is Leconte de Lisle's increasing consciousness of the attitudes of a society for which he would later write his own verse. If the year he spent as editor of *La Variété* reveals an inspiration that is diffused, it should be remembered that the young poet's apprenticeship occurred precisely at the height of the movement of social and utilitarian Romanticism which had begun to sweep France in the early 1830's. If he decried, with many writers of the time, the regime of Louis-Philippe for its corruption, he felt that literature and art could be the effective tools of remedy and reform. The new society, born of the French Revolution and an encroaching industrialism, could be redeemed by a widespread return to an idealism nurtured in some deistic context if not in any outright Christian princple. All of the young editor's writings are replete with hopeful and generous reference to the divinity. His subsequent loss of faith was to evolve from personal disillusionments yet to be encountered and from the new scientific spirit which imbued the age of Positivism.

After the failure of *La Variété* in 1841, Leconte de Lisle wasted little time in organizing and founding a new review, *Le Scorpion,* in 1842. But its scathingly satirical slant predictably incurred the displeasure of his uncle, the deputy mayor of Dinan, who relayed an unfavorable report to the family in Réunion. With his allowance cut off, and with no independent means of support, the young poet was compelled to abandon his new project and to return to his native island to seek employment in order to subsist. Having failed to obtain his law degree in Rennes, the young Leconte de Lisle had to content himself with the boring and menial tasks he was requested to perform for various business concerns in Saint-Paul and Saint-Denis. At odds with his family because of the manner in which he had spent his time in Brittany, he felt equally alienated from the planters and creoles with whom he was forced into daily contact. The years 1843 until 1845 proved to be a period of boredom and frustration for the poet who had little taste for business and economics. He grew to despise the creoles for their indifference to the hardship and suffering endured by the slaves who worked in the plantations. He crystallized his impressions of the creoles of Réunion in the story, "Saintive," where he recounts the abduction of a planter's daughter and the reaction of apathy rather than stoicism which the tragedy induced in the indolent natives. More a preachment than a serious attempt at fiction, "Saintive" denounced in unmistakable language the harshness of the creole and his blind indifference to the beauty which enhanced his existence: "What does the lustre of such incomparable nights mean to them? Things such as these can hardly be expected to find an outlet in the hearts of these European businessmen since a sun ray does not have the weight of a single sugar cane. The sight of the four walls of a warehouse is more susceptible of eliciting their pleasure than any glimpse of the largest horizon." [9] Bitterly resentful of the fact that his father kept slaves on the family plantation, the maturing poet managed to repress most of his anger while biding his time for an opportunity to leave his native island. Such an opportunity presented itself when friends from Rennes, recently converted to the Fourierist cause, invited him to come to Paris to collaborate on *La Démocratie pacifique* in 1845.

III Hope and Disillusionment

If nothing else, Leconte de Lisle valiantly contained within himself the urge to become a poet and a politician during the fourteen months he spent in Réunion. In his own mind, the realization of such an aspiration and vocation would have furnished him with a genuine sense of fulfillment and given him a complete and almost impossible happiness. As a member of the staff of the Fourierist daily newspaper, he would succeed in finding an appropriate outlet for the social idealism which had begun to overtake him. Under the direction of Victor Considérant, the staff and the collaborators of *La Démocratie pacifique* had as their primary mission the promulgation and expansion of the socio-metaphysical doctrines of Fourier who had died in 1837. Fourierism, which was founded in a vaguely defined Deism, was predicated on the somewhat abstract conception of generous fraternal cooperation which would give eventual birth to a future era of universal love and happiness. If the present times underscored an existence which proved to be less than ideal, these unsatisfactory conditions were the results of the errors of the past. With unflagging relentlessness, the daily editorials of the newspaper called for the wholesale commitment to the true cause of humanity by its predominanttly wealthy bourgeois subscribers.

Whatever may have been the likely reservations of Leconte de Lisle to some of the theses expounded by the Fourierists who constituted the movement around the newspapers, he found in their basic attitudes a justification for the need for harmony in the human hierarchy. What mattered most importantly was that the future poet found himself in the midst of congenial and sincere friends, all of whom aspired with unmistakable desire to see the end of the oppression of the poor.[10] What pleased him further was Désiré Laverdant's request that he become secretary to the editor of *La Phalange*, the monthly review which was associated with *La Démocratie pacifique*. *La Phalange* took on a more literary flavor since it purported to cater to the sensibilities of a more cultured clientele than the daily newspaper. The situation at *La Phalange* suited his tastes almost perfectly, and he ventured into the more personally rewarding realms of short fiction and poetry for his contributions to the Fourierist cause.

These were the years preceding the Revolution of 1848, and the feelings of hope for the future which they instilled in those who worked with tireless dedication for social remedies and reforms extended to Leconte de Lisle who contributed poems and stories which betrayed a discernible Fourierist tinge. "Sacatove" and "Marcie" are moving accounts, soberly conceived and executed, of acts and lives of veritable allegiance and devotion of two slaves at Réunion. These delicately related stories, rooted in nostalgia and recollection of his native island, succeeded in achieving a happy balance between a certain obviousness in theme and the art of storytelling. During the slightly more than two years he contributed to *La Phalange*, de Lisle published no less than fifteen poems, six of which were subsequently disowned by the poet in later years. Both the subject matter and the inspiration behind such lyrical pieces as "Hélène," "Architecture," "Niobé" and "Khirôn," for example, underline an evolution in thinking and expression undergone by the poet since his earlier association with *La Variété* in 1840. During his tenure on *La Phalange*, Leconte de Lisle had befriended such distinguished thinkers and writers as Eugène Maron, author of *L'Anathème*, a stimulating study on the French Revolution, Thalès Bernard, the noted translator who had just rendered into French the German Jacobi's *Dictionnaire mythologique*, and the brilliant Hellenist scholar, Louis Ménard. If Leconte de Lisle's poetry in *La Phalange* dutifully reflected, for the most part, Fourierist aspirations, the inspiration of his verses contained certain Hellenist strains which tended to stray further and further from references, however vague, to the traditional Christian deity of nineteenth-century France. The fact of the matter was that the poet's contact with such men as Thalès Bernard and Louis Ménard stimulated at once his imagination and his interest in the Greek past.

In the months that followed their first meeting, de Lisle grew especially fond of Louis Ménard, in all probability because he recognized in the latter's manner a genuinely profound respect for beauty and poetry. Ménard had just published a book entitled, *Prométhée délivré*, in which he argued that the plight of humanity was to suffer the oppression of tyrannies and witness the succession of dying religions. Prometheus' deliverance from such oppression, he continued, rested in the recognition that man alone was responsible for the redemption and the betterment of the world.[11] Ménard would later crystallize his thesis on the superiority of Greek polytheism over Christianity, yet it remains fairly evident that some of these ideas had already begun to filter down to the young collaborator of *La Phalange*. The truth of the matter was that de Lisle's most meaningful apprenticeship was taking place during these years which led directly to the Revolution of 1848. Louis Ménard was managing little by little to transfer the young poet's cult of beauty to a special cult for Ancient Greece. His success in accomplishing this task would prove invaluable to Leconte de Lisle: his espousal of the world of the Greek past prevented him from sinking into a sense of abject despair after the disillusionment he suffered resulting from the fiasco of 1848.

The so-called "Greek" poems which de Lisle contributed to *La Phalange* between 1845 and 1847 reveal the extent to which his attitudes had evolved since his initial encounter with Ménard. The poem, "Hélène," which appeared in 1845 and which de Lisle recast completely for inclusion in the *Poèmes antiques* of 1852, does not quite possess any inherently classical or pagan sense. Rather, the "Hélène" appearing in the pages of *La Phalange* is made to embody the Fourierist aspiration of a universal love and felicity. Similarly, "Niobé," which was published in the same year, betrays an almost Lamartinian faith in human emancipation. With "La Recherche de Dieu," however, which was included in an 1847 issue of the journal, Ménard's influence on Leconte de Lisle becomes more discernible: Rousseau's God has been replaced by a scientifically oriented appreciation of the function of religions in the evolution of man.

Despite the financial embarrassments he experienced during his association with the Fourierist group—as secretary to *La Phalange*, he earned only 150 francs per month—Leconte de Lisle was filled with hope and optimism. In point of fact, he had been nurturing illusions concerning the future of the France which envisioned a new and generous republic emerging from the Revolution of 1848. As a member of the Club Central Républicain, he had gone to Dinan in order to republicanize the ultraconservative inhabitants of this Breton city. All of his efforts in Brittany proved abortive. Still, undaunted, he gave his vigorous support to those who advocated the abolition of slavery in 1848. But the disappointing results of the elections in that same year and the bloody reprisals which characterized some of the June days which he observed destroyed his confidence in the possibility of a successful social revolution. The truth of the matter was that de Lisle only really managed to nourish a certain theoretical sympathy for the masses. If he would always adhere to a political philosophy which advanced the idea of social justice, he scarcely refrained from voicing his outright contempt for the people which he considered devoid of all meaningful principle. His letter to Louis Ménard on April 30, 1848, underscored his reaction in unequivocal terms: "The people are so stupid! . . . Let them die from hunger and cold. The masses are so easy to deceive; they will soon murder their only real friends." [12]

Whatever else, the experience of 1848 tempered most of Leconte de Lisle's enthusiasm for the Fourierist cause at *La Phalange*. Shortly after having been refused an appointment as professor of history at the Collège de Saint-Denis in Réunion, he volunteered his services as a collaborator to Lamennais's *Réforme*, but finally overcome with the conviction that all attempts at social reconstruction were doomed to failure, he disassociated himself from Lamennais's *Journal* as well as from *La Démocratie pacifique* and *La Phalange* in 1849. His disappointment in social and political matters doubtless increased the sense of dissatisfaction he felt since he had left Réunion in 1837. The resurgence of his pessimism from 1849 on was propelled by the sense of disillusionment and futility which befell him and those who had placed their hopes for a more just society in the short-lived Second Republic.[13] In a letter written on July 15, 1849, Leconte de Lisle recorded his disavowal of all practical and social concern in language which revealed the major attitude that he was to adopt and retain during the remainder of his personal and professional life: "Let's build ourselves a little hut in the forest of Réunion. We can be happy there. . . . We shall be honored there in our old

age, and when the time comes, we'll go together in Jupiter—
alas!" [14] The postscript to the letter summarized both the spirit
and the substance of the poet's newly adopted philosophy: "I
beseech you, old boy, do not allow yourself to get too bored.
Write some verse: it's the only way to be able to live a little." If
Ménard shared his friend's enthusiasm for the contemplation of
beauty, he remained nonetheless a scholar too much concerned
with the pressing requirements of the present to take the advice
seriously.

The Second Empire of Louis-Napoleon succeeded admirably in
replacing the idealistic void caused by the failure of 1848 with an
ardent new spirit which sought to reap the practical advantages
associated with the systematic exploitation of the applied sciences
and modern industry. The principally sentimental Lamartinian
faith in God had become supplanted by a surprisingly widespread
faith in the powers of science. The new discoveries in chemistry
and physics quickened the popular imagination which envisioned
a potentially limitless progress that would bequeath to society
great material posterity. The findings of such natural scientists as
Cuvier, Spencer, Lamarck, Darwin, Geoffroy de Sainte-Hilaire
and Claude Bernard, on the other hand, imposed a scientific
method whose adoption by leading thinkers and writers was
destined to revolutionize the modern approach to humanistic
problems. For the idealist who sought to bridge the gap between
materialism and spirituality, the chasm between the real and the
ideal grew still deeper. The distance separating aspiration and
belief extended itself even further. [15] Positivism, in fact, had ushered in the age of religious relativism, since beliefs would henceforth be placed under the same scientific scrutiny as all other
forms of human manifestation. By its very nature, Positivism
ignored all that which escaped natural observation, and so by implication at least, the new scientific method denied the existence
of any supernatural design in life. Hippolyte Taine described the
clash between faith and the new scientific method as "the paint-
ing of two different tableaus, one by faith and the other by science
which become increasingly dissimilar. The deep-seated contradiction between the two conceptions becomes flagrant by their very
development since each grows in its own way and in a direction
completely opposite from the other." [16]

Leconte de Lisle's response to the new intellectual and moral climate of the 1850's underscored the intricacy of the dilemma which many artists and writers felt compelled to confront. The drastic failure of 1848 constituted revealing evidence that a more exclusively historical approach to humanistic problems had already begun to supplant the largely abstract and dogmatic procedures hitherto in use.[17] Much of the pessimism associated with the works of Flaubert, Baudelaire and Leconte de Lisle, for example, proceeded directly from the insurmountable problems they encountered in attempting to adjust their respective idealistic stances to the predominantly positivistic philosophy which had begun to pentrate the France of the Second Empire. Their undeniable respect for science induced them to found their interpretations of the human predicament increasingly on the scientific observations of facts and on archaeological and even philological considerations. But the sense of anguish which pervaded most of their writing proceeded from the final inability to resolve satisfactorily the disproportion between their idealism and the limits such a scientific orientation explicitly imposed.

When Leconte de Lisle proclaimed the divorce of all pragmatic concern from literature in his preface to the *Poèmes antiques* in 1852, he was, in effect, admitting that the world would never be satisfactorily dominated by any specific political ideology. The anti-utilitarianism underlying both the preface and the poems which followed categorically rejected any accommodation made between art and industry in the name of science. With Flaubert and Baudelaire, de Lisle expressed his disgust over the awkward attempts being made by such inept writers as Théodore Weustenraad and Laurent Pichat to establish possible relationships between poetry and the new economic force. But construed mainly as an attack on the looseness and excessive sentimentality which characterized the Romanticism of Alfred de Musset, for example, the preface to the *Poèmes antiques* asserted itself with the kind of bluntness and aggressiveness which was bound to offend readers and critics alike. The essay, in point of fact, established Leconte de Lisle as a spokesman and a theoretician for the new literature which emphasized autonomy from moral and practical considerations and which encouraged the cult of art and beauty for their own sakes. In underscoring the urgent need to reexamine man's condition in the nineteenth century, the author of the *Poèmes antiques* proposed an itinerary for poets to follow in order to achieve the spontaneity and immediacy they so eagerly sought. The truth of the matter was that the prefaces to the *Poèmes antiques* of 1852 and the *Poèmes et poésies* of 1855 launched Leconte de Lisle's unofficial career as titular head of a new poetics which sprang from Art for Art's Sake to take on the official name in the 1860's of Parnassianism. The second paragraph of the preface which appeared in 1852 posed the problem which poets would discuss in *cénacles* and workshops and attempt to resolve. The optimism of the essay resides in its own programmatic appeal for the restoration of a lost primitive spontaneity in epic and lyrical verse:

In these times of uneasiness and of disquieting research, the best informed and the most sensible minds stop to consult with one another; the others remain ignorant both of their origins and destinies. They are swept along by the most feverish talk and exhibit little or no inclination for patience and quiet deliberation. Only the former betray any kind of awareness of the transitory character of their epoch and of the fatal exigencies which thus constrain them. We are part of a scholarly generation. The instinctive and spontaneous life, so blindly prolific during our youth, has left us: such is the unalterable fact. Poetry, which is fashioned in art, no longer inspires heroic action. Neither does it any longer inspire the practice of social virtue. This is so because its sacred language, despite the expectation of some latent heroism or virtue, has been reduced, as in all previous ages of literary decadence, to expressing merely impressions which are petty and personal and which are permeated by arbitrary neologisms. Poetry has been cut up into small pieces and rendered profane, and in its enslavement to individual whim and taste, it is no longer fit to teach man.

Leconte de Lisle makes it fairly evident that his new poetical code will strive to recapture the primitive spontaneity lost by an age imbued with new scientific spirit and dedicated to the cause of utilitarian progress. His entire concern from 1852 until his death in 1894 will henceforth center around the means to return to the veritable source and origins of the French poetic genius.

Founded in the exactness of scientific method and rigor, the verse of Leconte de Lisle attracted the attention of those who reacted similarly to the recent examples of Romantic sentimentality which had begun to contaminate French versification, robbing it of most of its immediacy. It was plain to most poets that French lyricism had slipped into some kind of torpor, and they expressed an eagerness to see it rescued from its virtual inanity. Slowly, and with varying degrees of enthusiasm, poets, such as Catulle Mendès, Xavier de Ricard, Théodore de Banville, Paul Verlaine, Théophile Gautier, Heredia and Leconte de Lisle, among others, responded to invitations of the publisher, Alphonse Lemerre, to read and discuss their verse in his bookstore in the Passage Choiseul in the early 1860's. But it was not until the beginning of 1864 that de Lisle managed to gather the kind of literary publicity to assert an informal leadership in the new movement.[18] He possessed a haughty and somewhat cold countenance, and his manner was very much that of an exacting taskmaster. The poets and friends who received invitations to his apartment in the Boulevard des Invalides on Saturday evenings prepared themselves for serious discusions on prosody and versification, the intensity of which was only slightly diminished by the frequent appearances of Madame de Lisle.

The three volumes of the *Parnasse contemporain,* which were published by Alphonse Lemerre in 1866, 1871 and 1876, are the collected verse of nearly one hundred poets of the time who elicited a decided sympathy with the aims and aspirations of the French Parnassian movement. Despite the lack of any precise literary principle or aesthetic code, the three editions of the *Parnasse contemporain,* to an important extent, pay tribute to the professed attitudes as well as to the leadership of Leconte de Lisle. All of the poets, published in Lemerre's anthology, remain united in their resolve to emancipate French lyricism from the bondage of nineteenth-century Utilitarianism. The particular practice of de Lisle's poetry, however, converging on the ideas of a possible redemption for modernism only through a return to the past, and the collaboration between art and science required for the purification and reinvigoration of poetic inspiration were, in the long run, attitudes immersed too deeply in a metaphysical pessimism for them to enlist any widespread popular response to such verse. The pessimism which ultimately overtakes his ambitious poetic program in such collections as the *Poèmes tragiques* of 1884 and the *Derniers Poèmes,* posthumously published in 1895, derived from his persistently gnawing consciousness of what Irving Putter aptly explains ". . . a disharmony between the poet's aspiration and the reality he encounters." [19] Such pessimism intensified itself as he encountered unhappy experiences in his personal as well as in his professional life. Severely criticized by his closest associates in 1870 for having accepted a modest pension from the private budget of Louis Napoleon in 1864, and having gained admission only with his third candidacy to the French Academy in 1886, Leconte de Lisle found little in life to dissuade him from a pessimism which had become deeply ingrained in him. He lived the life of a poet filled with expectant desires to be fulfilled. He suffered a final disillusionment for he had hoped to dominate life through art, and he ended by doubting the efficacy of his own work.[20]

CHAPTER 2

The Elaboration of a Poetic Creed

FOR Leconte de Lisle, the history of poetry remains inextricably bound to the history of humanity. As lovers and revealers of timeless beauty,[1] poets play both an historical and a religious role in rediscovering for nineteenth-century man the sources from which such beauty emanates. But such rediscovery can only proceed from the direction given by superior poets who have adamantly refused to surrender their veritable educational mission to the rampant pragmatic spirit of the age. In de Lisle's view, the individualism of Romanticism had failed, for the most part, to restore the lost primitive force and spontaneity necessarily characterizing all enduring lyrical expression. The essays which introduce such collections as the *Poèmes antiques* and the *Poèmes et poésies* do considerably more than expose the poet's conception of art and beauty; they also serve as practical guidelines for poets like him who sought the reform of the French lyric.

I *The Poet's Ideal Ambition*

Despite its aggressive attack on nineteenth-century cultural values, the preface to the *Poèmes antiques* of 1852 translated Leconte de Lisle's more pressing concern with evolving wider recognition and consciousness of the role played by lyrical expression in the social, political, and religious evolution of humanity. After labeling the nineteenth century as an age of decadence and degeneracy, de Lisle underscores the fact that the unbridled effusion, sentimentality, and capricious individualism which has come to characterize so much of the lyrical expression of the Romanticists has ultimately robbed it of its immediacy and effectiveness. Clearly, the situation of poetry in such a Positivist era cries out for urgent reform. In his desire to respond to the dated practical concerns and issues of an age bewildered by rapidly changing values, the Romantic poet strayed further and further away from his obligation as a guide for humanity:

Educators of the human race: the fact is that your disciple knows instinctively more about life than you do. He suffers from an inner torment for which you fail to provide any remedy and from a religious longing which you will be unable to fulfill unless you guide him in his quest for traditional idealism. Too, you will be compelled, at the risk of your definitive extinction, to withdraw from the world of action in order to take refuge in the contemplative and scholarly life as if it were a sanctuary of calm repose and of purification. Thus, by the very fact of your isolation will you be able to reenter intelligently into the real mainstream of your epoch without every straying from it again.

More than merely a criticism of some of the leading attitudes, de Lisle's statement emerges as a kind of blueprint of his own poetic itinerary. The solitary and contemplative existence which he reserves for the poet constitutes less an escape or a rejection of the world than a fundamental acceptance of the laws which rule and determine it.[2]

Creativity and poetic creation, in the purest sense of the terms, manifested themselves most abundantly during the era which produced Homer, Aeschylus, and Sophocles. The Homeric epic, in de Lisle's view, best exemplifies an ideal harmony achieved between man's material and spiritual aspirations. What he most deplores in nineteenth-century literature is the conspicuous absence of any truly epic dimension. Antiquity becomes quickly supplanted by a barbaric age which inescapably degrades and diminishes man's emotional, moral, and intellectual faculties. The legitimate aim and ambition of the modern poet is to rediscover through erudite methods the epic sense: "The genius and task of this century are to find again and to reassemble the sources and origins of the human intelligence." During periods of decadence, man allows himself to forget his vital past and readily succumbs to the new but dated dogmas which gradually strip the poet of his demi-urge powers. Through the accurate reconstitution of the past, de Lisle believes that man may return to his origins and refashion the model bequeathed by Antiquity. His advocacy of a spiritual return to the past asserts an acknowledgment of historical determinism, and his admiration for Greek Antiquity anticipates Renan's celebrated *Prière sur l'Acropole,* composed in 1865 and published in 1876,[3] in which a similar revelation of a perfect harmony between reason, beauty, and the intuition of the divine is conveyed in equally laudatory terms.

The preface to the *Poèmes antiques* condemns nineteenth-century lyricism as specious and sorely lacking in originality. Neo-Romanticism is nothing more than a desperate attempt at renewal which is doomed to abject failure. What alone is capable of restoring to poetry its lost primitive force and spontaneity is the devising and cultivation of clearer and more precise forms of expression. Only when a satisfactory formal reform manages to purify the mind and verbal expression of the defective practices which contaminate them will art truly recover its vigor, harmony, and essential unity. Leconte de Lisle concludes: "While awaiting for such a renascence to occur, it behooves the poet to collect himself in the study of his glorious past." The preface to the *Poèmes antiques,* to an important extent, is predicated on the hope that the acquisition of the force and spontaneity identified with Antiquity and Primitivism will be achieved at some future time. The preface to the *Poèmes et poésies,* written three years later, reaffirms this anticipation.[4] But Leconte de Lisle's expression of hope is conspicuously absent from the six studies which comprise the *Poètes contemporains* and from his *Discours de réception à l'Académie Française* in which he describes the three ages of man as the primitive, barbarous, and modern without any mention made of a possible return to the spirit of the Primitive age.

It should be underlined that when Leconte de Lisle subscribes to a return to the Greek past, he is ascribing greater importance to the historical and psychological conditions than to the cult of forms of that Antiquity. Central to his thinking on these matters is the conviction that it is imperative for the nineteenth-century poet to recover his lost powers and that the modern lyricist must attempt to recreate in him the spirit which inspired the classical epic. The advocacy of a return to the Ancients so that the poet might recover, through meditation and imitation, the spontaneity possessed by the primitive creators does underscore the necessity of abandoning the modern manner of thinking and writing. The study, adaptation, and imitation of the art of Greek Antiquity will instill in the poet the required inspiration, purify his soul, and thus render him accessible to the Ideal which he must contemplate and express. It results, somewhat paradoxically if not ironically,

that the desired recovery of a lost primitive spontaneity is ob-
tained from the exacting and rigorous exercises associated with a
certain cult of forms.

As a logical corollary to the idea that the poet return to the
spirit of Antiquity to rediscover true inspiration, Leconte de Lisle
proposed that serious efforts be made to unite scientific method-
ology with lyrical expression. The question had been raised by
other poets also, and Baudelaire's concluding statement on the
subject in his essay, "L'École païenne," which first appeared in the
January 22, 1852, edition of the *Semaine théâtrale*, underscored
the same attitude as de Lisle: "It is high time that literature steep
itself in a better atmosphere. The time is not far off when we shall
understand that any kind of literature which refuses to walk
fraternally next to science and philosophy is essentially a murderous or suicidal literature." [5] As "the reasonable study and enlightened exposition of external nature," de Lisle maintained that
science and scientific method recall the meaning of the traditions
which literature has dismissed and contribute to the restoration of
the forms which should characterize it. The prefatory essay to
the *Poèmes antiques* ends with the poet's recognition that the
pieces on Greek Antiquity will not likely elicit the enthusiasm of
the general French reading audience. Yet, de Lisle insists,
nineteenth-century ignorance of the past and its myths has given
birth to prejudice and misconception concerning the theogonic
explanations of Antiquity which prevent modern man from appre-
ciating the continuity of human aspiration. The *Poèmes antiques*
is offered as a modest endeavor to correct such misconceptions.

The tone and the defensive attitude discernible in the 1855
preface to the collection, *Poèmes et poésies*, bring out the fact
that Leconte de Lisle considered himself to be the main object of
Maxime Du Camp's attack on the conception of Art for Art's Sake
or Parnassianism in literature. Indeed, the preface to *Poèmes et
poésies* appears to have been composed as a counterattack on
both Du Camp's manifesto-preface and the pieces of the *Chants
modernes* which aimed to celebrate the alliance between art and
industry. Maxime Du Camp published his poems in honor of industrialism fittingly enough in the year of the Universal Exposition of 1855. With many others, Du Camp had rallied to a conception of poetry which had been inspired by the obvious ac-
commodations made by science and industry. If literature has

fallen into a sad state of decadence, maintained Du Camp, it was precisely because literature has turned backward rather than forward: "Science is making prodigious strides; industry is accomplishing miracles, and we remain unmoved, insensitive and scornful as we strum false notes on our lyres with our eyes closed so as to see nothing or to see with obstinacy a defective past that would be best forgotten. While the steam-engine has been invented, we continue to sing about Bacchus and bright red grapes. The whole thing is absurd!" [6] The thrust of Du Camp's prefatory-manifesto emphasized that a new world had been born from the union of science and industry and that literature inherited as its function to act as an interpreter of science and as a guide to industry.

The fact of the matter was that the question of the relationship between literature and industry was not a new one in 1855, and at various times, Baudelaire, Flaubert, and Louis Ménard as well as Leconte de Lisle spoke out in the most unmistakable language against any accommodation between art and industry. The harsh juxtaposition between rich industrialists and the poverty-ridden intellectuals was bound to engender a deep-seated resentment among the latter who scarcely refrained from registering their displeasure over such an exasperating situation. It was perhaps Ernest Renan, however, who underlined most succinctly the nature of the crisis of 1855: "For the first time [he is alluding to the Universal Exposition in Paris], our century has summoned the great masses of people without proposing to them any idealistic purpose. The ancient games, the pilgrimages, the tournaments and the jubilees have been replaced by the industrial fairs." [7] To a considerable extent, Leconte de Lisle's preface to the *Poèmes et poésies* constitutes somewhat of a psychological document on his own frame of mind as well as that of poets similarly concerned with the encroaching powers of the Industrial Age.

As evidenced by the critical reactions to the publication of the preface and the *Poèmes antiques* of 1852, Leconte de Lisle was being brought to task for advocating a pointless reconstitution of the Greek past. One critic in particular, Armand du Pontmartin, addressed this apostrophe to the author of the *Poèmes antiques:* "Do you realize what your fate—I was going to say chastisement —will be as a result of your efforts? Isolation." [8] Even Flaubert took exception to the tone of Leconte de Lisle's preface and voiced his objection over such an urgent insistence on returning to the Hellenic past. In a letter he sent to Louise Colet, Flaubert asserted: ". . . we should not attempt to revive Hellenism but rather satisfy ourselves with adopting its methods and procedures." [9] It is clear from the outset of the preface to the *Poèmes et poésies* of 1855 that de Lisle is anxious to clarify and explain the attitudes he advocated in 1852. The essay underscores the poet's appeal for a return to the epic past as identifiable with a constructive attitude for the future. Indeed, the future dignity of mankind rests on an intelligent assimilation and appreciation of Greek Antiquity rather than on any interest in the present which he considers to be an irretrievable loss. The preposterous alliance proposed between poetry and industry testifies to the reckless irresponsibility of the modern era.

The preface to *Poèmes et poésies* comes into sharper focus when Leconte de Lisle ventures to compare the Polytheism of Antiquity with the Monotheism ushered in by the Middle Ages:

In general, all that which constitutes art, morality and science came to an end with the death of Polytheism. Everything came back to life in its renascence, for it is only during that era that the idea of beauty reintroduces itself in the intelligence and the idea of right in politics. . . . It is not that I wish to insist at this juncture on the moral value of Polytheism in the social and religious realms. The study of this theogony, the examination of historical facts and institutions, the careful analysis of customs are sufficient evidence of a truth that can be admitted by any mind that is free of settled ideas and of uncontrolled prejudices. The art of Antiquity, alone, constitutes a revelation of such a truth. Henceforth, I shall limit myself to the world of art.

Of particular interest in Leconte de Lisle's comparison is the presence or inclusion of political philosophy. The opposition which he establishes between art and society is provisional, since in Antiquity as well as in the future he would like to anticipate, art, politics, and religion commingle.[10] Implicit in his comparison of the two religions is his condemnation of the Middle Ages

Leconte de Lisle pursues even further his argument in favor of the superiority of Greek Antiquity when he describes it as the only period in Western Civilization which successfully achieved the ideals from which a lasting lyricism had been able to proceed. "Poetry is at once generated by the intelligence, the passions and by reveries." By intellegince, he means the reasoned and intuitive comprehension of the universe. In the context in which it is described, passion becomes synonymous with obstinacy or perseverance in the realm of action, while the term, reverie, conveys an impression remarkably similar to that of the Romantic *mal du siècle*. Paganism's superiority over Christianity resides precisely in the fact that Greek art is characterized by an active concern for achieving the ideal, while Christian art appears content merely to evoke it and express a desire to achieve it. The order, clarity, and harmony achieved in the Ancient epics are only achieved by the classical Hindu culture. Leconte de Lisle's equation between the two cultures may be taken as an intimation as to the manner in which he will approach Indian mythology in his own poetry. The Indian poems which appear in his major collections play down the sense of the mysterious and of mysticism which impregnates Indian culture.[11]

In a review of the literary types created by Hellenic civilization, Leconte de Lisle declares simply that they will remain unsurpassed. Modern times have created nothing that may be said to approximate the unforgettable types of Antiquity. The feminine characters which find their way in the Greek epics typify ideal human types: they are complete since they belong at once to reality and to the world of dreams. By contrast, the types created in modern literature betray an incomplete conception of the ideal:

As for the creations of the poets that followed, they fail to fashion characters which are at once individualistic and general, and which contain within their actual individualities the complete expression of an idealized virtue or passion. And we could add, moreover, that the modern world manages successfully to conceive of feminine types only through alternations in their very essence, either by endowing them with manly characteristics as in the case of Lady Macbeth or Julie, or by relegating them to some nebulous and imaginary sphere as in the case of Beatrice.

What Leconte de Lisle decries in Dante's portraiture of Beatrice is not its obvious attempt at the idealization of womanhood, but its abstract symbolization of a theological force. Poetic and artistic idealization should proceed from reality as well as from the imagination. Beatrice's portrait conveys successfully the general type of a feminine force, but fails to suggest such a force in concrete and precise terms.

The preface to the *Poèmes et poésies* reiterates the poet's preference for Antiquity over Modernism because the Greek past makes meaningful reference to the youthfulness of man and his world and records the blossoming of a primitive force and beauty. Thus, Leconte de Lisle's advocacy of a return to the past is prompted by something stronger than admiration for artistic achievements that are superior to those realized in modern times. The fervent desire to know and recall his own origin and source motivates his ambition to study and recapture the lost flavor of Antiquity. Indeed, the pessimistic strain of his own metaphysical view of the world after 1848 receives considerable attenuation in his poetic and somewhat nostalgic recreations of a remote civilization whose most enduring expression celebrates an aspiration which is filled with hope and optimism.

II *The Achievement of Actual Poets*

Because he viewed the works of nineteenth-century French poets from the optic of his own poetic creed, Leconte de Lisle's critical appraisals of such poets as Barbier, Béranger, Lamartine, Hugo, and Vigny illuminate even further the principles which informed his own manner than those of his fellow lyricists. The studies which constitute the series entitled, *Les Poètes contemporains,* appeared in the review, *Le Nain jaune,* in the August, September, and October issues of 1864.[12] Conceived as commentaries on his contemporaries, de Lisle's essays stand as explicit repudiations of the Romantic aesthetic and of the proposed alliance between Beauty and Utility. The *avant-propos* is in a sense the affirmation of a poet seeking the approbation and admiration of his readers: "Art, therefore, Poetry is the brilliant, intense and complete expression of man. It is an intellectual luxury that is made accessible only to very rare and fine minds." De Lisle's tone is one of haughtiness and sarcasm; after berating the French for their enslavement to outworn clichés and attitudes, he concludes that ". . . the world of Beauty, the only real domain of Art is, in itself, an infinite having no possible contact with conceptions that are inferior to it." As with the earlier prefaces, the poetic creed proclaimed here is traversed by a certain optimism. In contrast with a metaphysical pessimism which underscored human limitation, a form of absolute was attainable through Art.

If it is true that the modern world remains devoid of art, the artist through diligent effort may succeed in rediscovering the lost paradise in a century or two, and spontaneity in the Greek sense will once against characterize lyrical expression. The true poet is he who perceives Beauty and who contemplates it so that he may be able to translate its expression accurately. The *avant-propos* assumes the tone of a manifesto in behalf of the necessity of endowing poetry with pure and impeccable forms:

It is in this spirit that I will study the work of contemporary poets. Above all, it is my intention to examine each poet as an artist, and I am certain that I will recognize a thinker and a high moral nature in each of them, even though it be not in the sense of the plebian intellectual. What I shall admire are the power, the passion, the grace, the fantasy, the feeling for nature and the metaphysical and historical comprehension of the universe—all of it expressed perfectly without which there is nothing at all.[13]

What Leconte de Lisle makes clear is the prime importance accorded to form which cannot be separated from subject matter. The formal exercises which he advocates so tirelessly that poets undertake in order to recapture the lost primitive spontaneity constitute a kind of expiation for the laxness which has come to permeate modern lyricism. In de Lisle's sense, form becomes not only a means of translating the ideal, but a means of achieving it.

Of crucial importance in these essays on nineteenth-century French poets are the conceptions Leconte de Lisle evolves on the nature of inspiration and self-effacement which invest his theory of literature with an undeniable optimism. The epic poets of Antiquity refrained from any conspicuous assertion of their personal predicament so that they might succeed in conveying as universal an expression of the ideal as possible. The dispossession of the self enabled the poet frequently to write effective verse which was endowed with an autonomous existence. To a remarkable degree, such a lyricist approached the supreme ambition of poetic creation. The impersonality assumed by the poet in no way implied the loss or surrender of the artist's consciousness. In a radical departure from the prevailing Romanticist belief that the poet was a kind of medium through whom the ideal passed, Leconte de

Lisle's position underscored the need for the lyricist to preserve his lucidity at the very moment of his inspiration. The question of appending analysis to ecstasy is analyzed in his essay on Victor Hugo:

The work of this man to whom all of us, who are possessed by a love of beauty and a hatred of banality, owe so much offers us the splendid example of the kind of virile individualism that emerges by sheer force and by leaps and bounds from hindrances that are common to us all. Hugo's work grows more certain each year as its sphere extends itself thanks to the magnificent overflowing of his intrinsic qualities as well as of his unusual defects, but which by their very nature continue to command our respect and veneration. With Hugo, we feel that we are in the presence of a powerful will which is conforming to its own destiny. And that is the mark of genius. In the world of art, in fact, the latent or conscious question of this definite accord constitutes the internal work which is a requisite for all well-endowed minds. The artist is complete when this agreement occurs.

Pursuing further this matter of poetic inspiration, Leconte de Lisle argues that spontaneity need not remain hindered by the poet's exercise of his will and his reflection. Quite to the contrary, he maintains, the conscious exercise of the will constitutes the best means of recovering the lost spontaneity. The acquisition of spontaneity results from the attentive and voluntary response by the poet to that which is most authentic in him. In his essay on Auguste Barbier, de Lisle declared that the task of the poet was to master himself as well as the world of chance and accident: "If the poet is above all richly endowed with extraordinary gifts, he is also the possessor of an intelligent will which must exercise an absolute and constant mastery over the expression of his ideas and sentiments, leaving nothing to chance and demonstrating complete self-domination insofar as that is possible." [14]

The *Poètes contemporains* affords Leconte de Lisle the opportunity of situating the poetic creed which he had evolved in the mainstream of nineteenth-century French literary tastes. If his criticism of his erstwhile benefactor, Pierre-Jean de Béranger,[15] may at first strike us as somewhat harsh and ungrateful, we should recall that Leconte de Lisle is appraising in this series not the art of the popular songwriter, but rather the art of the songwriter as poet. In the latter capacity, Béranger is viewed as completely lacking in originality which explains, de Lisle comments, why he enjoys such widespread popularity: "The author of the *Roi d'Yvetot* has not fallen into the public domain; he was born there, he lived there, and now, that is where he triumphs." The essay goes on to distinguish between Homer as a national poet and Béranger as a lyricist filled with patriotic sentiments. The greatness of the Greek poet rests on his ability to convey the mind and soul of the state, while the failure of the French songwriter as a poet proceeds from his obsession with the dated emotions and sentiments associated with political regimes.

The essay devoted to Lamartine may be seen as a kind of verification made by Leconte de Lisle to determine if the lyricist in the *Médiations poétiques* and the *Harmonies* conformed to his own conception of the model artist. Recalling his own addiction to Lamartine as the struggling editor of *La Variété* at Rennes in 1840, he catalogues him as a remarkable yet curiously incomplete poet who happened to write his verses at the propitious moment: "He came, sang and was adored." After dismissing the *Médita-tions* as a long musical lament which is badly rhymed, he proceeds to lavish considerable praise on the *Harmonies poétiques et religieuses* which failed to enlist the enthusiasm of the readers in 1830. De Lisle considers the *Harmonies* as better-constructed poems, technically, and better thought out, thematically, than the popular *Méditations*. His judgment of the collection betrays a haughtiness and contempt, however, for the general reader:

There are present here a lustre and a lyrical movement which are vastly superior to all that which is admired in the *Méditations*. The less resounding success of the *Harmonies* explains their higher artistic value. General approbation usually goes hand in hand with things whose best points offer no challenge to the common level. A poet can only expect to win popularity in France if he possesses the inexorable talent of being able to set rhymes to drinking songs or to extract a throbbing adventure from some vile lament.

Whatever reservations Leconte de Lisle may have communicated orally to his fellow poets concerning the efficacy of Victor Hugo's verse, the written commentaries which we have only underscore the greatness of his genius, singular praise, indeed, coming from such a caustic critic. Published in 1863, the essay on Hugo could conceivably have disintegrated into an attack on the

Utilitarianism preached by the exiled poet in his volume on William Shakespeare.[16] Despite the undeniable presence of both a political and messianic zeal in the verse of Hugo, Leconte de Lisle acknowledges him enthusiastically as the uncontested master of the French lyric. Viewed, however, from the perspective of the Second Empire, Hugo, in exile on the Channel Islands, is doomed to an obscure place in French letters by the Parnassian critic who prophesies wrongly: "Victor Hugo will never be a national poet." De Lisle speaks in eloquent defense of the comprehensive intelligence of a poet whose expression is a living force that bespeaks the marriage of reason and intuition:

The author of the only lyrical works of art which French poetry can present with the assurance of triumphant acceptance in foreign literature, this writer has restored to our rhythmical language the vigor, suppleness and lustre of which it was robbed for two centuries. He deserves the gratitude of poets and the respect of those rare minds who still understand and love Beauty. He betrays a certain excessive spirit which nobody will deny. He himself admits to it. There is, indeed, nothing but excess in *Les Rayons et les ombres, Les Contemplations* and *La Légende des siècles.* But what excess! I readily agree that the wholesome academic theories have little room for such excess. The fountains in our public gardens also display more restraint and balance than the volcanic eruptions. But, with proper timidity, I dare suggest that the latter provide a more thrilling sight than the former. We live in a temperate climate; we are honest and moderate; we are neither of a large or small stature, and we are impregnated with a Gallic common sense. But, alas, poetry is an excess of the spirit of which we never need feel guilty.

The remarkable kinship in personality and dominant attitude which linked Leconte de Lisle to Alfred de Vigny may be detected to a degree in the essay on the French Romanticist who retreated to an ivory tower. Such poems by Vigny as "Moïse," "Eloa," "Le Déluge," "La Colère de Samson,' and "La Mort du loup" are singled out by de Lisle as decidedly the most important and effective part of the Romanticist's production. The close spiritual alliance between Vigny's poems and de Lisle's "La Mort de Valmiki," "Qaïn," "La Vipère," and "L'Incantation du loup" provides the clearest clue for the critic's acknowledgment of the poet's great but somewhat defective talent. In a sense, de Lisle's essay on

Vigny constitutes little more than an exposition of his conception of the historical poem. And his explication of Vigny's bibical and historical recreations not always manages to eschew banality as in the case of "La Colère de Samson" which is summarily labeled "a very beautiful and complete poem." His judgment of "Moïse," however, displays greater discernment and affords him the splendid opportunity of contrasting Vigny with Hugo on the subject of historical reconstitution. "Moïse" is more of an intuitive re-creation than any really plausible account of the biblical legend, yet Vigny's poem goes considerably beyond the purely external aspects of history evoked by Hugo who portrays the hopes and aspirations of his own time in *La Légende des siècles*. Despite a purely individualistic interpretation of the story of Moses, Vigny's poem elicits the mixed admiration of the critic: "The poet's creation is altogether modern despite its historical or legendary aspect, and so consequently, it is factitious. But it is also human since nothing is human unless it belongs to the nineteenth century, certain persons called critics would venture to say. No matter. As long as the verse is beautiful, and it is frequently magnificent."

Leconte de Lisle bespeaks his disapproval of the artist who would let himself be overtaken by the moralist in him in the essay on Auguste Barbier. The latter subscribed to an alliance between poetry and morality which, in the critic's view, accounts for his failure as a lyricist since his verse can hardly be construed as more than rhymed didacticism and a negation of poetry. Leconte de Lisle takes up again his definition of the poet as educator, distinguishing between the poet who reveals Beauty and the writer who reveals truth:

As soon as he succumbs to the deplorable temptation of taking to the pulpit, the artist dies in the poet and he is of no use to anyone, for there exists no other efficacious teaching except in art which has no other purpose but itself. There is no salvation whatsoever except through the creation of beauty. Only the incompetent profess instead of creating works of art. They ignore or appear to ignore that the beauty in a verse is independent from any moral or immoral sentiment, however people may choose to understand these terms, and that the verse expresses and requires, in some ways, a special extra-human quality.

*   *   *

Immorality, in de Lisle's sense, is the betrayal of the idea or concept of Beauty by dated concerns or unworthy formal expression. Barbier was impregnated with a sense of the beautiful, but failed to express it adequately and effectively.

The strength of Leconte de Lisle as critic rests on the explication of his fundamental affirmation that the primary function of poetry is the expression of Beauty which should provoke the sentiment of joy in him who reads and contemplates its expression. In such instances, he manages to clarify and deepen the principles which inform his own poetic creed. As analyst of the works of his contemporaries, he often fails to comprehend the subtleties and intricacies which characterize their respective lyrical conceptions. His critical dogma is directly posited on his own idea of the function of poetry, and his critical essays on his contemporaries represent an attempt to judge them by the standard which he set for himself.

Elected a member of the French Academy on February 11, 1886, only after presenting his candidacy for a third time, Leconte de Lisle's acceptance discourse was nervously anticipated by many who feared that he might attempt to denigrate the memory of his predecessor, Victor Hugo, or to vent his disgust with the present state of literature in France.[17] The *Discours de réception à l'Académie Française*, delivered on March 31, 1887, actually took up again the most salient features in attitudes he had expressed in the prefaces and in the *Poètes contemporains*. The address constitutes a remarkably clear synthesis of his own poetic creed. De Lisle prefaces his supposedly laudatory remarks on Victor Hugo by an insistence that historical circumstances determine whether or not artistic genius may manifest itself at given times in the cultural development of a nation. The speech is, in effect, a chronological appraisal of the entire literary production of Hugo, and the new academician lavishes praise on his poetry which he labels as sublime. The closing paragraphs, however, underscore the ideological differences which separate de Lisle from his predecessor in the French Academy:

All of his life, he evoked a supernatural dream and apocalyptic visions. He is obsessed with the eternal mystery. He proclaims a disdain for science which attempts to explain the origins of life, and he even refuses to grant it the right to attempt an explication. In this, he is guided more than he admits to be by the arbitrary dogmas of revealed religions. He believes he draws from his deep faith an infinite power, at once remunerative and merciful, and a generous compassion which animates him in behalf of the weak, the disinherited, the wretched and the outlawed to whom he offers asylum so nobly. It is his duty, he believes, to convey in sublime language the beauty, grandeur and harmony of the visible world as the splendors of a future humanity, and he refuses to recognize that he owes his magnificent conception of Beauty only to his own genius just as he owes his outbursts of goodness and generous indulgence to his own heart.

Despite their divergencies in outlook and method, Leconte de Lisle's explanation of Victor Hugo's inspiration betrays at least an indirect attempt to slur the reputation of nineteenth-century France's most widely acclaimed lyricist. Edgard Pich underlines with particular aptness that Hugo does indeed draw his compassion for the oppressed from his faith, even though the object of that faith may possibly not exist.[18] The *Discours de réception* strays at several junctures from the guiding principles of Leconte de Lisle's critical approach: that the critic define the nature of the artist and that he verify to ascertain that the works submitted conform to his ideal model.

CHAPTER 3

The Poèmes antiques

THE preface to the thirty-one poems comprising the original edition of the *Poèmes antiques* in 1852 made it clear that the "exercises" in celebration of past civilizations had scarcely been designed to appeal to readers who considered poetry as little more than sentimental recollections or personalized reveries. As the foremost exponent within the Parnassian movement of a poetic neo-Hellenism, Leconte de Lisle doubtless benefited from Victor de Laprade's versified interpretations of ancient myths in such works as *Psyché* (1841) and *Odes et poèmes* (1844). It should be remembered that de Lisle's growing enthusiasm for Antiquity became further solidified through frequent conversations with the brilliant scholar of Greek civilization, Louis Ménard, who spoke of the possible renascence of a type of evolutionary paganism that could adjust to the requirements of modern civilization. Leconte de Lisle's recourse to the remote past in the *Poèmes antiques,* then, can hardly be described as innovative. Yet, his obsession with Hellenism, for example, in the collection possesses little in common with the more scholarly and practical ideas on the matter of his mentor, Louis Ménard. Rather, it was founded, like the literary antiquarianism of Théophile Gautier, in an interpretation of objectivism which camouflages a decidedly personal reaction to human experience.

As a series of documented studies on Antiquity, the *Poèmes antiques* purported to illustrate the alliance between poetry and science which Leconte de Lisle believed was capable of purifying lyricism of the elements which contaminated it. Richard Chadbourne has aptly described what the lyricist of the *Poèmes antiques* understood as science to be the acquisition of a positive historical knowledge and especially that of past religious phenomena.[1] The fact of the matter was that the social and political events of 1848 served as such corroborative justification for his own pessimism that he sought officially to disassociate himself completely from what he considered disdainfully were the dated and pragmatic concerns of nineteenth-century civilization.

If the majority of the poems comprising the *Poèmes antiques* may be considered as the offspring of his own sensitivity, it should be added that de Lisle sought eagerly to objectify his conception of an idealized Antiquity with the external accouterments of a seemingly objective and scientific approach. His notion that the contemporary reader stood to benefit most from the examples of past civilizations which came closest to achieving the human aspiration toward beauty, harmony, and unity stemmed in large measure from his own rejection of all values associated with the society in which he lived. It is no exaggeration to say that the greater number of the *Poèmes antiques* conform more readily to the poet's own dreamworld than to the factual world of Ancient Greece and India. What he felt could no longer be achieved in his own times, Leconte de Lisle sought to achieve through the artful and idealized reconstructions of the remote past. Such an endeavor confers upon the most successful poems of the collection an undeniable lyrical dimension. The charges of impassibility and impersonalism which so many critics are willing to append next to his poetic production attest most eloquently to the fact that Leconte de Lisle's verse still manages to convey to readers that it is essentially lyrical expression which is tempered and authenticated by a serious concern for historical and scientific data.

The definitive edition of the *Poèmes antiques* which appeared in 1874 included some twenty-five additional pieces, most of which were transferred from the *Poèmes et poésies* of 1855 by Leconte de Lisle, who decided to eliminate the latter collection from the work.[2] For the purpose of our analysis of the volume, let us say that the *Poèmes antiques* may be divided into three distinct categories: namely, the Greek poems; the Hindu poems; and the miscellaneous poems. The three cycles of lyrics receive their fundamental unity from the poet's celebration of an idealized beauty which he identifies with past civilizations or with an exotic nature far removed from the immediacies of the nineteenth century.

I *The Greek Poems*

Such poems as "Niobé," "Hélène," "La Vénus de Milo," "Khirôn," and "Hypatie," most notably, which had appeared previously in the pages of *La Phalange* as lyrical symbols of the Fourierist conception of an earthly harmony, are divested in the *Poèmes antiques* of all allusions to any contemporary ideology, and join the other poems as expressions of admiration of the Greek notion of love and beauty. The short epic, "Khirôn," for example, underscores the evolution which had taken place in Leconte de Lisle's attitude from the days of its initial publication in 1847 to its revised appearance in the *Poèmes antiques* of 1852. As a three-part epic poem, "Khirôn" recalls the old centaur's visit by Orpheus before whom he begins to sing the praises of the Giants who took up arms against the god, Zeus. Khirôn knows that he has been condemned by "the pale Olympian gods" and awaits calmly and stoically his own murder at the hands of the young Héraklès. To a significant extent, "Khirôn" looms largely as the nostalgic recollection or evocation of a primitive time in which the earth had not yet been daunted by the cruelty of capricious gods. De Lisle's centaur, Khirôn, is riddled by doubt and torn by anguish because he is aware that the Olympian gods represent no absolute since they are the fabrications of a people. Orpheus, who holds the torch of poetry, listens in sadness to the centaur, who describes a desire for domination and eternity within him which can neither be squelched nor assuaged:

And I, as a witness to such prodigious times, while I pitied the vanquished, I applauded the gods, for I was then certain that they were just. Yet, there burned within me a dark secret engulfed as in a flame. As I sat by the flowing waters, I frequently allowed my thoughts, filled with terror and with doubt, to wander. Dreamer! I would say to myself. There is on the snowy crests an eagle who is able to spread his stormy wings and whose eye is constantly fixed upon the sun as he repeatedly attempts to break the stress of the winds in the bewildered space. He knows that his strength is hidden in this eternal struggle, and he derives satisfaction from it. Greedy for light and thirsty for battle—for the earth remains dark and the skies remain low—he soars and ascends into the skies and struggles as his avid claws seize the three-pronged lightning whose fire consumes him.[3]

* * *

The Poèmes antiques

In the 1847 version which appeared in *La Phalange*, both Khirôn and Orpheus recall the destiny of the Romantic poet, a collaborator of the divinity, who leads the people toward progress and instills in them a sense of the ideal. As he appears in the *Poèmes antiques*, Orpheus becomes the intermediary who would attempt to invest the hearts of men with some measure of reassurance. Behind his mythological reconstruction, Leconte de Lisle raises a very personal issue in "Khirôn" which will continue to plague and haunt him during his entire career as a poet. To a degree, the poet shares the centaur's predicament since he is also possessed by the same gnawing desire for the absolute which Khirôn is compelled to dismiss as a fatal and logical fabrication of the human mind. In his monumental study of Leconte de Lisle, Irving Putter explains that the poet's pessimism, ostensibly couched in a somewhat erudite or scholarly framework for the most part, stemmed from the religious relativism which issued from the philological and archaelogical discoveries of the scientific age: "It was a principle of pessimism for Leconte de Lisle. He was neither a materialist nor a theoretical philosopher who could be content with faith in some abstract principle." [4] The *Poèmes antiques* as a whole betrays an implicit if not always explicit nostalgia for a past that is no more or for a love and a beauty whose ideal expression is identified with youth or primitivism. The pensive centaur in "Khirôn" identifies the happiest years of his existence with youth's initial aspirations: "How beautiful I thought the Earth was while I was young! In those days, the silt of the great waters turned the highest mountain peaks in the Aither region green again." [5] Leconte de Lisle's treatment of mythology in "Khirôn" sets the tone for the majority of the poems which constitute the Greek cycle.

One of the most prevalent tendencies among critics and literary historians has been to identify Parnassian poetry with such terms as plasticity, materialism, and verbal description. There can be no denying that such a practitioner of Parnassianism as Leconte de Lisle was moved to evolve a cult of the beautiful in art and literature in reaction to the abusive exploitation of the imagination by some of the leading Romantic poets. To a significant degree, the differences which separated Romanticists from Parnassians proceeded from the manner in which they chose to respond to the riddle of man's enigma. Faced with the dilemma of reconciling the contradiction which existed between the unlimited human aspiration and the narrow limits imposed by reality, the Romanticists elaborated explications more inextricably bound with intuitive feelings than founded in the observation of any external reality. Their language bespeaks an ethereal and vague quality which attempts to translate the metaphysical world rather than the physical one. The leading proponents of Art for Art's Sake and Parnassianism, on the other hand, faced the same dilemma in a more sober and scientific manner. Benefiting from the Positivistic methods introduced during the opening years of the Second Empire, they favored attitudes issuing from the factual observation of the external forms of reality. If Romantic optimism may be described as unfounded in fact, what passes for Parnassian pessimism receives its corroboration from the historical evidence that the riddle of the human enigma remains an insoluble one. Such Parnassian poets as Leconte de Lisle excluded any outright subscription to a spiritual explanation of man's predicament since they adhered officially to an attitude which sought a more factually oriented and materialistic interpretation of the human condition.

In his determination to avoid the cosmogonic and metaphysical interpretations of the Romantic poets, Leconte de Lisle advocated that lyrical expression be made to rest on the more scholarly and objective approaches to art and beauty. The poet, then, shared at least a procedural bond with the scholar and the scientist of the Positivistic age insomuch as he sought to extract his art from the systematic observation of concrete facts and reality. His consequent transpositions of the elements of lasting beauty which he discovered in the material world favored a type of verse which was far more descriptive than it was suggestive. The cult of beauty in art proceeded from a desire to reconcile the real and the ideal. Such a cult, in fact, prevented his pessimistic views from emerging with any overwhelming or categorical force. If the Parnassian poet disclaimed any possibility of reconciling man's finite nature with any sense of the infinite, the cult of idealized beauty which informed his art permitted him to seek out at least a partial solution to the human dilemma. The very fact that he felt helpless to explain satisfactorily man's persistent aspiration toward permanence frequently induced him to inject an implicit personal ingre-

dient in his descriptions of the beauty which he associated with
the concrete world.

On one level, the poem, "La Vénus de Milo," which appeared in
1852, takes on an almost programmatical role as the expression of
the Parnassian ideal of enduring beauty and harmony residing in a
concrete manifestation of Greek Antiquity. The ten stanzas constitute a visual celebration of the untainted purity and beauty
which the sight of the statue of the Vénus de Milo stirs within the
contemplative poet. The images which emphasize the statue's
perfection endow the poem with its unifying aesthetic coherence.
Leconte de Lisle subtly blends the concept of such lasting beauty
with the idea of a superior civilization in this poem which may be
taken both as a description and an evocation of physical or concrete perfection. Indeed, the images used to convey the sense of
permanence which Leconte de Lisle associates with the statue are
infused with a nostalgic longing for the Antiquity which encouraged this material yet artistic embodiment of man's notion of
eternity. The closing lines of "La Vénus de Milo" translate the
poet's cult of art and beauty in language that borders on the
religious:

Island, sojourn of the gods! And you, Hellas, my sacred mother! Why
could I not have been born also in the holy Archipelago during those
glorious centuries when the earth was truly inspired and could see the
heavens descend at its first urging! If it is true that my cradle has
never been caressed by the flowing waters and the mild crystals of the
ancient Thetis, and that I have never prayed to you, Victorious Beauty,
at your native altar under the Athenian façades, ignite me, nevertheless, with your sublime spark so that my glory might not be enclosed
with me in my anxious tomb. Allow my thoughts to trickle in golden
rhythms like a divine metal in an harmonious mould.[6]

Central to any serious claim of objectivity and impassibility in
the *Poèmes antiques* is the degree of historical authenticity with
which Leconte de Lisle manages to describe and evoke Antiquity.
Most scholars and critics agree that the Greece which is conjured
up in these poems is actually an idyllic Antiquity which corresponds more to his own psychological needs as an artist than to
recorded historical fact.[7] In other words, his Greece is a poeticized
Greece which one critic has characterized as an earthly paradise
in which the harsh light and the dryness customarily associated

with the Mediterranean climate are conspicuously absent.[8] Thus, "Thyoné" may be more accurately described as a rearrangement or a personal adaptation of Theocritus' poem. Leconte de Lisle invests his version with a certain languorous quality which makes his shepherd more indolent and given to reverie than the original Greek counterpart. The truth of the matter is that poems such as "Thyoné" bespeak a virtual independence from their specific Classical sources. To speak plainly, the Parnassian poet remains above all a poet. The *Poèmes antiques* translates a personal frame of reference, and the Greek context in which de Lisle places his meditations on life and art rescues his lyricism ultimately from precisely the type of effusion he sought to avoid. Examined closely, the poems which comprise the Greek cycle scarcely attempt to mask the poet's personal philosophy or vision of the world. If "La Vénus de Milo" and "Le Vase" may be accurately catalogued as exalted expressions of ideal physical beauty, "Thyoné" is a commentary on the frigidity of women, while "Glaucé" and "Klytie," for example, may be called portraits of women in love and of desired women, respectively. These are themes which Leconte de Lisle will continue to exploit under different guises in subsequent collections of poems. All of them originate in a personal viewpoint which he will attempt to reconcile with his evolving conception of art and beauty.

There exists perhaps no better single piece of evidence delineating the mental anguish suffered by Leconte de Lisle as a result of the religious relativism which asserted itself in France during the reign of Positivism than the poem, "Chant alterné," which had undergone substantial revision from its first appearance in the June, 1846 edition of *La Phalange* for its inclusion in the *Poèmes antiques*. Cast in the form of a dialogue between two interlocutors who are designated merely as roman numerals I and II, "Chant alterné" is a celebration of both the Pagan and Christian ideals such as they were manifested in their initial vigor and glory. The mood established through the dialogue is one of nostalgia for the irretrievable past. Led by an irresistible drive for knowledge, modern man recognizes through his spirit of inquiry that the new scientific age has replaced absolute ideals by a religious relativism. In other words, the Positivistic age has put an end to the dogmatic spirit. The final three stanzas, or verbal encounters, of "Chant alterné" convey the sense of loss which the poet experiences since, as a poet, he appreciates the value of the Pagan and Christian ideals which have since become devitalized by the modern attitude.

II. When the wise men began to hesitate, the soul closed its wing, and men bid the heavens a sad and dismal farewell. I had eternal hope germinate in him, and I guided the earth to his God!
I. Oh! sensual delight, the cup of flowing honey from which the earth quenched its thirst! The world was happy then, and it was filled with immortal song. Your beloved daughter, lost and alone, now sees only the grass of neglect and forgetfulness grow upon her altars.
II. Love, unstained love is like an imperishable flame. Man has closed his heart, and the world is now orphaned. Will you ever be born again from the night of your soul? Will there ever be a single dawn that knows no sunset? [9]

The poems, "Hypatie" and "Hypatie et Cyrille," which made their way into the definitive edition of the *Poèmes antiques* of 1874, illustrate, once again, how Leconte de Lisle made use of history and legend to convey with seemingly more objectivity a stance or an attitude which remained at least partially rooted in his own subjective response to experience. The historical Hypatia, a scholar of mathematics and astronomy of considerable prestige in Alexandria, had been charged by the bishop Cyril with having instigated and encouraged the persecution of Christians in 415 A.D. A citizenry whose anger had been provoked by the bishop's accusation had Hypatia beaten and burned at the stake. In both poems, Leconte de Lisle has fashioned the historical Hypatia into the symbol of a dying pagan civilization. The poet's sympathy for the pagan martyr stems, in large measure, from his conception of history. He professed the view that religions, like the myths and legends which translate the aspirations of different people in different milieux, do affirm, particularly at their apogees, elements of an eternal human truth and ideal. The sadness projected in both poems emanates from de Lisle's realization that the imminent extinction of Greek Polytheism underscores the irreconcilability of man's limitless aspiration and his limited achievement. The evolution of history attests to the fact that as old myths, legends, and religious beliefs become discarded by societies which have grown more complicated and sophisticated, new myths, legends, and religions emerge in response to the psychological climates created in such societies. The process is thus an endless one.

Leconte de Lisle's emotional identification with Hypatia rests in the fact that, for him, she represents the last though futile expression of faith in an ideal. He associates Hypatia's faithfulness to the gods with an undying allegiance to the cult of beauty. The 1858 poem, "Hypatie et Cyrille," presents the two protagonists as antithetical forces: Hypatia symbolizes a humanity which is endowed with an impulse toward permanence and absolute beauty, while Cyril conveys that attitude which would brutally rob men of their dreams. Hypatia, then, incarnates, through her appreciation of a superior civilization, a nostalgia for an heroic conception of humanity, and Cyril becomes the embodiment of a pragmatic reality which is vile and reprehensible. There can be no mistaking the fact that Leconte de Lisle considers Greek Polytheism a superior expression of religious belief to Christianity. What particularly appealed to him, as a poet, was the intimate bond established in Greek Pantheism between an aspiration toward the divine in the human mind and nature rendered divine through the cult of the beautiful. What de Lisle abhorred in Christianity was its sense of the practical and its apparent indifference to beauty. Hypatia's nurse lashes an indictment against the fanaticism which seeks the destruction of knowledge and art so unremittingly:

No. I tell you that I have heard only too well their barbaric clamor. I am not in the least mistaken. They all damn you as they invoke your name. Their hearts are furious and their faces are inflamed; my dear daughter, they will tear you to pieces. These monsters are in rags, and like revolting animals, they go about predicting all kinds of evil. Riddled with desire and burning with envy, they blaspheme beauty, light and life itself! [10]

Leconte de Lisle made no attempt whatsoever to squelch his repulsion for Christianity which he held to be an inadequate religion for the requirements of the nineteenth century. From the perspective of his religious relativism, he judged the value of a given religion by the quality of art and poetry it inspired in its adherents.[11] But Christianity, by only increasing human anxiety, fell considerably short of the artistic merits and fulfillment of Classical Greece. Much of the effect or impact of "Hypatie et Cyrille" is considerably reduced by the discursive tone of the final section of the poem. Cast in the form of four dramatic scenes, the declamatory tone of the confrontations between protagonist and antagonist divests much of the emotional appeal which such a dramatic meeting of opposites should incite in the reader. Hypatia and Cyril emerge, in the end, as personified allegories of knowledge and fanaticism which engage in a kind of philosophical debate on the cultural worth of Paganism and Christianity. Nonetheless, the final speeches of the third and fourth scenes translate in particularly effective terms the nature of the poet's own stoical attitude with respect to his role and function in society.

I cannot allow a cowardly silence to induce me to forget that for the sake of my own honor I have a supreme task to accomplish. I must proclaim and confess proudly and openly under the skies the beauty, truth and goodness which the gods have revealed to me. Since two days now, the barefooted monks with their unkempt beards and their dirty hair, looking emaciated because of their fasts, and sunburned, have been leaving the desert and swarming into the city like a vile scum. People say that a sinister and fanatical design brings this hysterical horde into our midst. That may be so. But I know how to die, and I am proud of the choice with which the gods have honored me for a last time. I am, nevertheless, grateful to you [Cyril] for your concern, and only request that I be given a few moments alone.

[Scene IV. *Hypatia addresses her nurse.*]
"I shall be immortal. Farewell!" [12]

II   *The Hindu Poems*

We have seen how Leconte de Lisle, who reacted with disgust to his own times, turned toward the Greek past in whose idealization he sought to replace a philosophical void by a purely aesthetic appreciation of that civilization. The poems on Hindu culture which he included in the *Poèmes antiques* were hardly intended to contribute to the vogue of interest in Eastern philosophies during the 1840's. The fact of the matter was that the metaphysical interpretations of existence expounded in Hinduism and Buddhism fell in nearly perfect accord with his own views and feelings. It is perhaps not an exaggeration to say that Leconte de Lisle sought in Indian impassibility or apathy an explanation and a refuge for his own disillusionment and sadness. His study and observation of human experience—youthful ardor, passionate love, and religious institutions—underlined the inevitable passing of man's most pressing and urgent desires. If aspects of Indian philosophy detectable in Lamartine's *La Chute d'un ange* (1838) elicited his curiosity, Eugène Burnouf's *Introduction à l'histoire du Bouddhisme* (1844) and the translations of the sacred Hindu texts proved to be nothing less than a revelation to him. The Buddhist view of human existence as suffering corresponded to his own feeling on the subject which he had been endeavoring to articulate in his poetry up to this time.

Despite the remarkable similarities that exist between Schopenhauerian pessimism and Buddhist doctrine, it remains highly unlikely that Leconte de Lisle had been able to read the German philosopher in any systematic fashion since French translations of the *Aphorisms* appeared only in 1880 and the treatise, *The World as Will and Idea,* from 1888 through 1890.[13] On the other hand, translations of such sacred texts as the *Râmayama* and the *Rig-Veda* were made available in the 1840's and doubtless made a significant contribution to the growing interest in Ancient Indian civilization during that time. Central to Buddhist thought was the concept of *nirvana,* a kind of absorption into nothingness and the supreme deliverance from suffering, the inherent condition of all human existence.[14] Leconte de Lisle's own pessimistic views sprang from the realization that human life was but a desire for eternity and the absolute which was destined to remain unfulfilled. Desire, then, was but a goad for something which man could never really hope to attain. Hence, his suffering. To escape the anguish of such a fate would require a recognition in him that the object of his aspiration is inane. Such an attitude necessarily negates the universe as a positive state in which the gratification of human desire is sought. It was primarily the ideal negation of the personal will and movement in the Buddhist sense of *nirvana* which attracted Leconte de Lisle to Eastern thought and philosophy.

Paradoxically, the state of *nirvana* or absorption into nothingness could only be realized through the practice of virtue and through the vigilant attention of the individual.[15] The final apathy achieved is the result of concentration and meditation. Absolute negation, then, of all subject and object requires an effort of purification within the individual as well as the practice of six transcendental virtues. Leconte de Lisle's interest in Buddhism betrays no evidence that he ever attempted to fulfill any of the requirements which purportedly would have enabled him to achieve the desired final apathy.[16]

In point of fact, the Hindu subjects constitute little more than masks or objective frameworks for the poet's own attitudes in much the same manner that the Greek subject matter enabled him to express his actual reactions to life without resorting to the kind of overbearingness and effusion which marred the verse of so many Romanticists. Like Vigny before him, Leconte de Lisle sought out the philosophical implication of his own experience before he attempted to transpose it into his poetry. In such Hindu poems as "Sûryâ" and "La Vision de Brahma," for instance, his account of India is more poetic than it is rigorously factual. Scholars and critics are generally agreed that de Lisle often altered elements in Ancient Indian legends, and syncretized aspects of Buddhism and Brahmanism to have his subject matter conform more actively to the requirements of his poetic imagination. Such modifications, to an important extent, harbor Leconte de Lisle's personal revelations. Just as in the Greek poems, the Hindu pieces give the lie to the charge by certain literary historians that de Lisle's verse bears the imprint of impassibility and impersonality.

"Sûryâ," which was written for the original edition of the *Poèmes antiques* in 1852, illustrates Leconte de Lisle's frequent disposition to fuse elements from completely different sources and traditions. Bearing the subtitle, "A Vedic Hymn," "Sûryâ" juxtaposes aspects derived from the *Rig-Veda* with other mythologies. Scholars point out that if "Sûryâ" were strictly speaking a Vedic hymn, the sea, which underscores an important motif in the poem, appears nowhere in the sacred texts of the *Rig-Veda*. In Vedic mythology, Sûryâ was the sun god who had been abandoned by his mother, the goddess, Aditi. Wandering in the heavens in a chariot drawn by seven yellow horses, Sûryâ sought feverishly to regain his rightful place among the gods. This Indian legend appealed to Leconte de Lisle whose "Sûryâ" may best be described as an exalted hymn of praise to the elemental forces of nature. The plight of the sun god, condemned to recover his lost primitive force, incarnated, in many respects, the predicament of the poet who sought to recover a lost spontaneity and power far away from the crass concerns of an utilitarian society. The refrain, repeated no less than four times, evokes the life-giving waters and identifies them with the life-giving power of the mother, Aditi: "Master, your abode is on the shores of the ancient oceans where the great waters come to wash your mystical feet." [16]

"La Mort de Valmiki," [17] which was added to the *Poèmes antiques* in 1881, translates with eloquent concision the poet's expression of an absolute faith in the immortality of art. Reworked from an episode in the Hindu epic, *Mahâbhârata,* it recounted the death of an ascetic enveloped in his dreams and spirit of penance. Leconte de Lisle replaces the ascetic, Tchayana, by the father of Sanskrit poetry, Valmiki, whose life was shrouded in legend. A Brahman by birth, the epic poet retreated to a life of meditation in the womb of nature far from the worldly cares of his fellow men. The skeleton of his body was recovered some one thousand years later by Indian wise men. Presumably he had been devoured alive by millions of white ants. Leconte de Lisle's account of the incident in "La Mort de Valmiki" affords him the splendid opportunity of conveying a quasi-religious affirmation of the endurance of a work of art in a world in which everything is doomed ultimately to be swallowed up in a great void. Contained such as it is within the larger structure of the narrative account of Valmiki's horrible death, the statement on artistic immortality achieves a stunningly antithetical effect with the pervading mood of the poem:

For the spirit no longer perceives anything about the senses nor about itself.

The long slimy termites, dragging their white bellies, undulate toward their inert prey around whom they gather and circulate, and into whom they sink down and swell like the rising sea foam. They swarm over his feet, his thighs and his breast as they bite into and devour his flesh. They penetrate the cavity of his large head through the eyes, and they become engulfed in his purple mouth which is open. They transform this living body into a stiff skeleton propped up on the Himavat mountain like a god on his altar. That was Valmiki, the immortal poet, whose harmonious soul continues to penetrate and fill the shadows in which we find ourselves. His words will forever remain on the lips of men.[17]

The long narrative poem, "Bhâgavat," traces the itinerary of three wise Brahmans who seek to return to the origin of all life and to lose themselves in the breast of a nature that has mothered all men. If it is true that Leconte de Lisle's account owes more to his own poetic imagination than to any erudite reconstruction of Hindu wisdom,[18] the somewhat rambling aspects of "Bhâgavat" enable him to project his complicated assimilation of Ancient Indian philosophy. Conceived as a mixture of evocations of nature and of invocations by Maitreya, Narada, and Angira to the goddess of nature, Ganga, "Bhâgavat" unfolds the steps necessary to accomplish their return to the original source. In the opening part of the poem, we encounter the three wise men in the midst of the murmurs and noises of wild birds and animals who simply ". . . were meditating, while they sat in the reeds." [19] The three Brahmans represent, through their respective invocations, three different attitudes to existence. Maitreya is the lover who pursues the dream of an inaccessible ideal, while Narada experiences contentment because he has broken completely with worldly concerns. Angira is the beleagured metaphysician who remains painfully conscious of the irreconcilability of faith and reason: "I have lived with my eye fixed on the source of all Being, and I have allowed my heart to die in order to know and understand better." [20] The three Brahmans recite an harmonious lament concerning the defective nature of man to Ganga:

The human lament is the cry of an anguished soul and of a heart that endures torture. Who can hear you without quivering from love and pity? Who can refrain from weeping for you, magnanimous weakness, human spirit which a divine goad excites and wounds, but which ignores you while you cannot hope to attain it. And, now, you shall never be able to limit this unreachable goal during the human night which appears endless to you. Will you be able only to embrace the Infinite in a sublime dream? You are a painful spirit which is carried off into space while you thirst for light and are hungry for beauty. You always fall from the divine altitude where each living soul seeks its origin. And overcome by sadness and terror, you groan; for, who weeps for you, vanquished conqueror? [21]

When the goddess, Ganga, appears, she informs the Brahmans of the power of Nature to absorb men within her bosom. The three wise men begin the ascension to the mountain of Kaîlaça beyond which they hope to find the land of the origin of all life. Various gods appear to them along their journey, and when finally they perceive Bhâgavat, the Brahmans ask but to absorb themselves in him, and escape from the carnal prison which imposes limitation upon man's life. In the end, all remains motionless for in such repose comes deliverance from the inconsequential activities of a world in constant flux. Irving Putter has judiciously pointed out that the inert Brahmans' conscious rejection of life in "Bhâgavat" proves to be all the more dramatic and astonishing because everywhere around them in the poetic account, life swarms with an unremitting restlessness.[22] What the Brahmans ultimately experience in this state of indifference to worldly concerns is a feeling of the divine void or *nirvana*.

Bhâgavat, you smile upon these sublime souls for it was you, as the powerful God, dispenser of all good, who untied the spirit from its supreme link. And now, all three of them are united in your limitless bosom, the ocean of light, and the first Essence which is the beginning and the end, the truth and the error, and the abyss of nothingness and of reality. The invisible Maya, creator of the world, the embodiment of hope and recollection, of dreams and of reason, envelops all men forever with her fertile flame. Such is the only, the eternal and the sacred illusion.[23]

Much of the lyrical effectiveness of "Bhâgavat" derives from the poet's adept integration of Hindu mythology and thought with his own reactions to the human predicament.

Like the other verse which comprises the Hindu cycle in the *Poèmes antiques,* "La Vision de Brahma" achieves considerable success in masking the personal ingredient present in this poetic reaction to man's metaphysical problem. To an extent, Brahma's position with respect to the all-powerful God which he interrogates recalls the position of Christ with respect to God the Father in Vigny's poem, "Le Mont des Oliviers." In both cases, the protagonists serve as thin disguises for the poets in question. Moreover the doubt with which Brahma and Christ are invaded translate through clever indirection the uncertainty experienced by Leconte de Lisle and Vigny. Brahma, like Vigny's Christ, is puzzled by the contradiction implicit in the idea of a troubled and imperfect creation emanating from an omnipotent and perfect Creator. He articulates such a question before the God, Hâri, because he hopes somehow that the contradictory elements may be reconciled. Hâri's answer is that the divine void is the only reality which exists, and that such a void is only vaguely conscious of itself in much the same manner in which dreams vaguely allude to reality. The solution to man's anguish rests precisely in the fact that such anguish should be transcended by forgetfulness and self-effacement:

Brahma! such is the dream in which your spirit is engulfed. Question no longer the august Truth, for, what would you be without my own vanity and the secret doubt of my sublime nothingness? And on the golden summits of the divine mountain of Kaîlaça where white genies swim in pure air, the inexpressible Voice stopped its harmonious flow, and the terrible but holy vision vanished.[24]

Critics reproach Leconte de Lisle for having confused "La Vision de Brahma" with an indiscriminate combination of Brahmanism and Buddhism which invests the poem with a disquieting element.[25] Buddhist thought precludes any belief in a Supreme Being, and Brahmanism never makes allusion to nothingness. "La Vision de Brahma" is Leconte de Lisle's own statement on the nature of man's tragic search for the absolute.

III *The Miscellaneous Poems*

The presence of such well-known poems as "Midi" and "Dies Irae," grouped under the rubric "Poèmes diverses," underscores the fact that if Leconte de Lisle persisted in projecting his own pessimism into his work, he avoided remarkably well the pitfalls of uniformity and monotony of presentation. Not the least effective verse of de Lisle are the so-called elegiac and descriptive nature poems. However subtly he manages to camouflage his personal feelings, de Lisle remained a poet who could not be content with the mere presentation of scenes and situations. Such poems as "Midi" and "Nox," for example, convey the personal conception of a majestic and mysterious nature whose contemplation inspires him with a strange yet undeniable detachment and alienation. For all its power and beauty, nature remains something which is indifferent to the needs of man. This idea had been introduced by Vigny, coincidentally the French Romanticist with whom Leconte de Lisle expressed the greatest affinity. Much like his Romantic counterpart, his observations of nature confirmed the pessimism of his metaphysical attitude. With Vigny also, Leconte de Lisle is predisposed to judgment in his representations of nature. Poems

such as "Midi" reveal the presence of a powerful imagination behind the plastic descriptions of a minutely observed scene at high
noon.

"Midi" emerges as something considerably more than another
visual celebration of the sun as a source of life and energy; it also
projects a commentary on the relationship between man and nature which conforms to the poet's personal metaphysical views.
Whatever emotional balance is achieved in the poem results directly from Leconte de Lisle's ability to describe in such con-
vincing terms a scene which depicts the hot noonday sun beating
down relentlessly on a plain and adjacent forest in what presumably must be a French countryside. The opening strophes, through
their recurrent reference to images which emphasize a blazing
white light which envelops a motionless cornfield, establish the
mood for the meditation which terminates the poem. And that
meditation proceeds naturally from such notions as heat, immobility, engulfment, and light which are evoked and which penetrate his descriptions: "silver sheets of light fall at noon," the
fields are entirely without shade," "an overwhelming heat," "the
earth sleeps in its dress of fire," and "the air burns without the
slightest breeze: everything is silent." If the scorching noonday
sun invades the surrounding landscape with an oppressive heat,
the "white" oven which lie in the slopes adjacent to the cornfield
remain oblivious to all which surrounds them, and appear absorbed in some deep dream. What is particularly felicitous in
"Midi" is the remarkable way in which the poet conveys an
illusion of reality. The oxen, for example, are described in a characteristic pose which is made to coincide ingeniously with the
philosophical attitude which is finally spelled out in the closing
strophes.

The conspicuous absence of man from the purely descriptive
tableau in "Midi" invites the poet to address him directly. Such
explicitness, however, does not detract from the unity of presentation in the poem, since Leconte de Lisle uses this device primarily
as a ploy to infer his message as unobtrusively as possible. There
is a lesson for man to infer from the description of a becalmed
nature and oxen whose inertness bespeaks numb contentment.
The animals respond intuitively to nature unlike man whose
instincts have become blunted by his excessive concern with the
requirements of a modern society. The last four strophes encour-

age the prospective onlooker to immerse himself in the tableau
of blissful serenity before returning to the lowly cities:

And close-by, a few white oxen lie on the grass and slowly dribble on
their thick dewlaps. Their magnificent, languid eyes appear to be following some inner dream which they never finish. Man, if someday
you come upon these radiant fields at high noon with your heart
bursting at once with joy and bitterness, then, run away! For nature
remains indifferent and the sun consumes everything in sight; there
is nothing alive here, nor is there anything that is sad or joyful. But
if you are disillusioned in your laughter and in your tears, and if you
thirst to forget this troubled world, not knowing anymore how to
forgive or how to damn, and you wish to experience one last pleasure
in numbness, then, come! The sun will address you in a sublime language. Try to absorb yourself endlessly in its unrelenting ray, and go
back slowly toward the lowly and despicable cities with your soul
seven times soaked in the divine void.[26]

Despite its classification by Leconte de Lisle as "a miscellaneous poem," "Midi" may be joined logically to the cycle of Hindu
poems in which aspiration toward nothingness and the divine void
is underscored with an unfailing consistency. The nineteenth-
century French critic, Sainte-Beuve, singled out the closing
strophes of "Midi" for the sudden shift in emphasis which complicated the nature of the descriptive tableau.[27] It is precisely such
a complication which lends Leconte de Lisle's statement on the
indifference of nature to man such a feeling of overriding pessimism in "Midi." He went considerably beyond such poets as
Vigny and Hugo, who exploited a similar theme in their lyricism. If anything, "Midi" asserts the idea that nature is the
crucible in which the Darwinian struggle for survival occurs.
Unlike his Romantic predecessors, however, who bewailed nature for its apparent indifference to human needs, Leconte de
Lisle sees in its impassibility a lesson which can prove to be
beneficial to the poet torn by the relativism of the age. If nature
does not exactly represent the exteriorization of an inner human
aspiration toward permanence, it does contain an appeasing
quality which enables the poet to desire an ultimate absorption
in it. Too, insofar as it invites man to seek a psychological deliverance from the painful limits imposed by given societies at

different moments of history, nature restores to man that peace of mind which the pressing preoccupations of unsatisfactory social organizations have destroyed. The pessimism pervading "Midi" issues from the implication that all modern societies fail to respond to the most urgent needs of the individual.

The bitterness with which Leconte de Lisle conveys his pessimism stems precisely from the fact that he entertains nothing but the darkest and most abject notions of modern society. Unlike such thinkers as Renan and Louis Ménard who attenuated considerably their respective conclusions on religious relativism with active concerns for social and intellectual progress, the author of the *Poèmes antiques* refused to view human existence except through the idealistic vision of the consummate artist.[28] Nowhere is such an attitude asserted so categorically as in "Dies Irae," the poem which concludes the collection. The title of the poem—Day of Wrath—is borrowed from the thirteenth-century Latin hymn which has since been incorporated into the Catholic liturgy for the dead. Within the ostensible framework of a meditation, "Dies Irae" conveys the vision of the total annihilation of mankind. What rescues the poem from disintegrating into an emotional apostrophe is an exemplary balance between a personal and an historical view of the human predicament. Leconte de Lisle evokes the aspiration of youth, the golden age of civilization, and his own bitter disillusionment with remarkable mastery and control. Yet, there can be no mistaking the abject pessimism which the poet's acknowledgment of the displacement of God has engendered in him. Man's only appeasement lies in his dream of a return to his original state of nonbeing:

Where are the promised Gods, the ideal forms and the great cults clothed in velvet glory? And where is the white ascension of the serene Virtues into the heavens which open their triumphant wings? The Muses, like divine Mendicants, go slowly by the cities as they find themselves the prey of a bitter laughter. After enough blood has trickled from under the headband of thorns, they give out with a sob that is as endless as the Sea. Yet, eternal Evil reigns in full power! The air of the age proves bad for cankered hearts. Forgetfulness of the world and of the multitude, we greet you! Nature, take us back in your sacred bosom.[29]

*   *   *

Formally and thematically, "Dies Irae" summarizes superbly the nature of the Parnassian poet's defection from the modern world of relativism.

Critical and popular reaction to the *Poèmes antiques* proved, for the most part, to be negative. The belligerent tone of the preface, as well as the exploitation of themes unfamiliar to the general readers, predisposed an unfavorable reaction. On the whole, reviewers reproached Leconte de Lisle for emphasizing motifs which so scathingly denounced all contemporary values. Of the entire collection, only "Midi" won any kind of enthusiastic endorsement. But in a general way, there was a decided recalcitrance even among the most sympathetic analysts to consider the Hindu poems as serious lyricism. Be that as it may, the *Poèmes antiques* won an honorable mention in the annual awards day of the French Academy in 1853. And at least one of Leconte de Lisle's congeners in Art for Art's Sake hailed, without reservation, the success of the Hindu lyrics: Théophile Gautier, in a perceptive notice subsequently published in the 1884 edition of his *Histoire du Romantisme,* praised the cycle for conveying so admirably the Indian sense of *nirvana*.[30] What the *Poèmes antiques* underscored beyond any doubt was the ascendancy of an important poet on the French scene.

CHAPTER 4

The Poèmes barbares

WHEN they first appeared in 1862, the *Poèmes barbares* bore the unfortunate title of *Poésies barbares,* and critics unsympathetic to Leconte de Lisle scarcely refrained from commenting wryly if not ironically on the nature of his "barbaric verse." The initial edition comprised but thirty-six poems, the majority of which had been published earlier in such journals as the *Revue des deux mondes,* the *Revue contemporaine* and the *Revue européenne.* By 1872, the name of the collection had been changed to the *Poèmes barbares* in order to parallel more closely the title of the *Poèmes antiques.* The definitive edition of 1878 included some seventy-seven poems, with the significant increase accounted for by Leconte de Lisle's decision to redistribute the lyrics from his *Poèmes et poésies* of 1855. Thematically, the *Poèmes barbares* continues where the *Poèmes antiques* left off. The wider range of topics covered in the new volume underscored further the poet's exploitation of different myths and legends to convey his personal reactions to human experience.[1] The formal rigor which characterized his verse and the recourse to history and legend served as an objectifying filter for the actual emotions that are betrayed in the *Poèmes barbares.*

By the term *barbare,* Leconte de Lisle understands all of that which is not representative of Greek and Indian Antiquity. Chronologically speaking, Barbarism in de Lisle's view extends down to the time just prior to Modernism. If Classical Antiquity represented the highest achievements of man, the Barbaric epochs, despite all of their harshness, were still judged preferable to the Decadence of the nineteenth century. From Xavier Marmier's *Chants populaires du nord* of 1842 and Léouzon-le-Duc's translation of the *Kalevvala* in 1845, de Lisle managed to enlarge his own vision of primitive civilizations from the perspective of his personal prejudices. His *Poèmes barbares* mourn perceptively the disappearance of all civilizations, for in spite of the fact that reason taught him that the idea of permanence was but an illusion, he revolted temperamentally against such a conclusion. His poems record the Nordic legends with significant changes and enlargements; he frequently creates an ambience in which energy or a vital instinct is made to coexist with tenderness. The men, animals, and nature which adorn the *Poèmes barbares* more often than not evoke man in his primitive state.

Leconte de Lisle classified the *Poèmes barbares* in 1862 according to a chronological and geographical order starting from Biblical Antiquity down to the Nordic Middle Ages. For the purpose of our examination, we will adhere generally to Joseph Vianey's classification of the poems according to subject matter.[2] Under the all-encompassing rubric of "barbarism," we shall divide the majority of the poems into the following cycles or categories: Nordic and biblical legends; jungle or animal poems; love lyrics; nostalgic nature poems; the Middle Ages; and Modernism. In each of the above categories, the poet's personal feelings stamp the most representative and successful lyrics with the undeniable mark of a true poetic dimension. By and large, the lyrical quiver running through the *Poèmes barbares* is an implicit one since, on the surface, these poems strive laboriously to convey an impersonal attitude.

I *Nordic and Biblical Legends*

Implicit in the various myths and legends concerning Finland, Iceland and the Scandinavian countries, which were translated and published in France during the 1840's and 1850's, was the notion that the fall of these ancient cultures began from a marked decline in spiritual idealism and from a widespread acceptance of material values. Given his personal views on modern society, no subject could have appealed more directly to Leconte de Lisle, and he proceeded to underline such a motif in his poetic renderings of these Nordic tales. Much of the lyrical flavor detectable in the poems which constitute this cycle stems directly from the manifest attitude which dictated his treatment of the various folkloric and epic accounts of the civilizations in question. His reading and consequent adaptation of Léouzon-le-Duc's translation of the *Kalevvala* in the poem, "Le Runoïa," for example, illustrate the manner in which he sought to blend source materials with feelings and reactions which resided completely within himself.

Leconte de Lisle's poem, "Le Runoïa," recalls that portion of the *Kalevvala* which relates the displacement of the old Finnish religion by Christianity in the middle of the twelfth century. The conflict emerging between the two religions gave rise to numerous myths and legends at the time, with some accounts underlining a peaceful or nonviolent resolution of the situation, and other sagas asserting a vigorous resistance to Christianity. "Le Runoïa" is based on the harsher version found in the *Kalevvala* in which the Finnish god, Runoïa, provokes a hostile encounter with the Child who represents the new religion. Such as he is presented in de Lisle's poem, the Runoïa resembles more a ruler than a god. As king of the northern reaches, he is endowed with certain Orphic powers which inspire the runes, magical and prophetic writings which provide spiritual direction for the people. Unlike in Léouzon-le-Duc's translation of the Finnish epic, the Runoïa of the *Poèmes barbares* is surrounded by poet-priests who possess stone harps and by hunters. It is evident from the outset of the poem that Leconte de Lisle is enlarging upon both the setting and the story line in order to spell out with greater dramatic force the theme he has selected to develop.

The landscape setting evoked in "Le Runoïa" conveys the presence of a savage and elemental force. There is a sense of grandeur which emanates from the poet's portrait of a violent nature in which the snow, the hail, and the winds somehow suggest a conspiracy with inhabitants who should exhibit a concomitant energy and drive. In a deliberate deviation from his source materials, however, Leconte de Lisle replaces the Runoïa's intrepid warriors by degenerate hunters. The latter display a reckless lack of concern for the matters of the spirit and prefer to revel shamelessly in materialistic comforts. There can be little doubt that the poet saw in the Runoïa's hunters the counterpart of nineteenth-century man who had disowned idealism for materialism. The Runoïa reads his fate as he listens to his hunters who disinherit themselves of the heroism bequeathed them by their ancestors.[4]

Let them [past beliefs, etc. . . .] die if they must! If they do, will we be able to hunt the lightfooted stag any less in our native steppes?

Let the day predicted by the fatal runes come! The quarrel between the gods constitutes no danger to us so long as the wily bear continues to be ensnared in our traps and so long as the overheated hydrometer does not break the bow! . . . Brothers, life is good under the heavens! Let us live, and open up our hearts to new intoxications! To be able to drink and to hunt in peace: those are the only good things that exist. Let us drink! Our blood is hot, and our women are beautiful. Tomorrow has not yet arrived, and the past is nothing.[5]

The hunters lack vigor and they bespeak an indifference and lethargy which Leconte de Lisle implies is only matched by the Barbarism of modern times. But the center of "Le Runoïa" gravitates around the interview which takes place between the Runoïa and the Child. The poet makes it explicitly clear that an even worse Barbarism will succeed the old order, for Christianity asserts itself categorically against the aspirations of reason and nature. The religion of the Runoïa will be succeeded by a religion which negates the naturalistic life and is devoid of all joy and beauty. "Le Runoïa" conveys a certain nostalgia, for the poet regrets the passing of any religion or civilization which has succeeded in fulfilling a measure of human aspiration. In a real sense, the poem registers Leconte de Lisle's personal disapproval of Christianity as a beneficial religion. The broken Runoïa, representing the annihilated materialistic cult of the Finnish deity, turns to the victorious Child and prophesies the eradication of Christianity in language that betrays the poet's own feeling in the matter.

Alone, the eternal Runoïa descended into the midst of this tremendous ruin in silence. Now dispossessed of a world, he launched his bronze iron-bottomed boat on the sea. And as a strong gust of wind suddenly twisted the white tuft of his royal beard, his eyes gazed fixedly on the remains of his tower, he let out this scream into the night: —You shall also die in your turn! I swear nine times on the immortal runes that you shall also perish like me, god of a new soul and spirit. For it is written that mankind will survive you! You shall for twenty centuries inflict pain upon man and cause him to bleed and to be reduced to tears until the day when your yoke, which he shall have endured for two thousand years, will break the neck of the mutinous races. Then, your temples, erected in the various nations, will become the butt of mockery for generations. And your hour will come, too! You will return to your mystical heaven covered in an ascetic's shroud as you

leave future men in their indifference and in their old age fall asleep as they blaspheme the gods!—
And, as he swam in the foam and the clang of the abyss, he disappeared as he faced the sublime space before him.[6]

Leconte de Lisle relates a similar opposition between the forces of an outmoded Paganism and a new Christianity in the poem entitled, "Le Barde de Temrah." Drawing heavily from Hersart de la Villemarqué's *Légende celtique en Irlande*, published in 1859, and from general history,[7] he succeeded in avoiding in his account of St. Patrick and the Druids the antithetical presentation of "Le Runoïa," whose thematic explicitness destroyed much of that poem's lyrical effectiveness. Despite minor changes made with the legendary story, de Lisle manages to conserve throughout "Le Barde de Temrah" a certain thematic unity which endows the poem with a felicitous air of authenticity and subtlety that is seldom encountered elsewhere in his production. "Le Barde de Temrah" recalls Patrick's trumphant entry into the Ireland of the ancient Druids. The conflict residing between the two religions is conveyed by a certain tension which sets the forces of nature in opposition to the powers of the spirit. Such an opposition is evoked from the opening lines and is sustained throughout the poem, and it leads naturally to the dramatic confrontation which ultimately takes place. Patrick, the representative of Christianity, is "the pale and mysterious stranger," while Murdoc'h and his entourage, the representatives of Druidism, wear "crowns which interlace wood from the oak tree with leaves of holly." As the two religious attitudes converge, the horizon stands still for a crucial moment, and the earth and the heavens appear to withdraw into an inert sleep. When a new light emerges in the skies, a subdued and subordinated nature is born. This is symbolized by an allusion to the dawn and the birds who collaborate in a spirtualized harmony in honor of the new deity. Christianity has displaced Druidism, and Patrick goes about baptizing the inhabitants of Ireland in the new religion.

In Leconte de Lisle's source material for "Le Barde de Temrah," it is a relatively minor personage, Milcho, who resists the exhortations of Patrick and who prefers suicide to surrender. In La Villemarqué's *Légende celtique en Irlande*, Ossian is won over to Christianity by the missionary. The poet of "Le Barde de

Temrah" alters the original fictional account so as to make the hero of his poem a pagan. Indeed, the complex antagonism which exists between Patrick and Murdoc'h, the symbol of an heroic if futile resistance to Christianity, provides the poem with its central focus. What the poet has set out to underscore is much less the repressive character of Christianity than the unbreakable bond that attaches man to nature. The confrontation between Patrick and Murdoc'h takes place appropriately where "reptiles crawl under thorn-bushes and sea-hawks and owls emerge plaintively from the great empty shell nearby." [8] The ensuing debate reveals that Murdoc'h's resistance to Christianity is prompted by an ingrained sense of loyalty to the heroic if doomed tradition of his ancestors. If Patrick's entreaties concerning redemption go unheeded, it is because this last resisting Druid aspires to be reclaimed, like his ancestors, by the land of his birth:

At these words, the old bard straightened up, took the sword, and with his two hands plunged it into his heart. Then he fell against the hard ground, saying: —Friend, tell your God that I am rejoining mine.—Thus, the bard of Temrah, Murdoc'h with the long hair, died as he dedicated this bloodied offering to the dark Spirit, so says the holy legend. Then, the palace in ruin became suddenly illuminated by ghastly fires from which there emitted horrible sounds. The bard had rejoined his ancestors as he had wished it. Remaining next to the body whose soul, alas, was still alive, the Apostle knelt and sorrowfully pleaded for Murdoc'h, but God refused to grant his fervent petition. Murdoc'h's remains were consumed by the eagles and the wolves.[9]

In "Le Barde de Temrah," Leconte de Lisle has succeeded in conveying in eloquent language a message which he has imparted elsewhere in his verse with considerably less effectiveness. The success of the poem doubtless rests in the poet's manifest sympathy for the two protagonists in his account of the Irish legend. "Le Barde de Temrah" displays exemplary formal control and mastery over a difficult theme. The fact that de Lisle refrains from indulging in his predictable denunciations of Christianity has prevented this poeticized version of Patrick's advent into Ireland from being sidetracked into a distracting diatribe. The poem's unity remains intact throughout. "Le Barde de Temrah" reveals the sense of inadequacy which all men experience when the two opposing powers of matter and spirit assert themselves with such categorical force. This is a conclusion which underpins Leconte de Lisle's pessimism.

The manner in which the poet of "Le Coeur de Hialmar" fashioned verse possessing artistic cohesiveness from sources as varied as "Le Chant de mort de Hialmar" and "Le Chant de Regnar Lodbrock" from Marmier's *Chants populaires du nord* speaks eloquently in behalf of the undeniable fact that he never allowed his inspiration to be smothered by any apparent erudition.[10] "Le Coeur de Hialmar" is a particularly appealing visual or plastic evocation of the stoical heroism of a primitive Scandinavian warrior. In its vivid alternation of scenes which depict life and death, the poem achieves a certain epic quality which is hardly expected in verse of such short length. The scene which is depicted is that of a somber battlefield just after an awful battle has taken place. The eerie light of the moon, the cold wind, and the flight of vultures above the field blend admirably with the gruesome sight below of thousands of motionless bodies which lie in pools of blood. De Lisle succeeds from the beginning of this poem in achieving a highly visual impression by a deft handling of the verbal and the expressive points of the text.

With one last burst of energy, the wounded Hialmar, feeling the murmur of death within him, calls out to his motionless soldiers who are stretched out on the battlefield. After he has realized that he alone remains alive, he implores a nearby raven to open his heart and take it to his fiancée, the daughter of Ylmer, in Upsala, so that she may be assured of his undying love for her. Leconte de Lisle establishes an association between the courage of the barbarous warrior and the instinctive rapacity of the scavenger. There is nothing mawkish about the heroic warrior's monologue: Hialmar's speech has the ring of harshness and directness which translates a soldier's language. There can be no denying that the love he openly professes is a simple and ennobling one. The almost metallic texture of the words he employs in his entreaty is marvelously attuned to the harsh evocation of death in "Le Coeur de Hialmar." For all of his obvious barbarism, the dying warrior conveys an admirable courage and a rare sense of primitive grandeur. As he faces death stoically, he is haunted only by the love he experiences for his fiancée. His last wish is only that she look upon him as a heroic warrior who goes forth boldly to take his place in the sun among the Scandinavian gods.

The Poèmes barbares

The alterations which Leconte de Lisle fashioned from his source material point out the fact that it is primarily through his creative imagination that he has woven this artistically successful evocation of a barbaric and primeval epoch which probably never really existed in actual fact. What renders "Le Coeur de Hialmar" beautiful as narrative verse is the spell which is cast from the first evocation of darkness in the opening strophe and which is maintained until the final evocation of light in the concluding strophe.

The richness of detail which is so much in evidence throughout "Le Coeur de Hialmar" invests the descriptive tableau with both an epic and a sculptural motif. Such motifs make it possible for us to translate the warrior's barbaric proposition to the raven as the expression of an innately pure and noble heart:

Come here, Raven, my brave scavenger of men's flesh; open my chest with your beak of iron. You will still find us here tomorrow just like we are now. Take my warm heart to Ylmer's daughter. Go to Upsala and fly as swiftly as your wings will allow, prowler of the heather, to where the Jarls [Scandinavian noblemen] drink good beer and sing in chorus as they clink their golden pitchers. Search for my fiancée, and carry my heart to her. . . . Go, messenger of death, and be sure that you tell her that I love her very much, and give her my heart. And when she sees that it is still red and firm, and not trembling and pale, the daughter of Ylmer will smile in gratitude at you! As for me, I shall die. My spirit flows beyond life in the twenty wounds that I have received. I have lived my life, and my time is up. Wolves, drink my crimson red blood. I go to take my place among the gods in the sun as a young, brave, laughing, free and untainted man! [11]

Like such notable forerunners of Romanticism as Byron, Goethe, Hugo and Nerval, Leconte de Lisle was tempted to recast the story of the first rebel in biblical times, such as the tragedy of Cain related in the fourth through the sixth chapters of Genesis. The poem, "La Fin de l'homme," which appeared in 1858, sketched the notion of man's revolt against the injustice of an essential universe arising from the Judeo-Christian tradition. To an extent, "La Fin de l'homme' may be considered as the prelude to the more ambitious epic verse, "Qaïn," in which de Lisle attempts to portray both the beginnings of a race and its awesome annihilation in the Great Deluge. The entire story is recounted from the timeless perspective of the seer, Thogorma, whose dreams recall the genesis of man in the Garden of Eden, and prophesy the doom of an entire race in the Flood. The opening strophes of the poem establish an antithesis between the people of Iahvèh (Jehovah) and the pagans who lived shortly after the creation of man. Iahvèh's people are pictured living in fear and in dismal submission to a capricious and vengeful God who answers their entreaties with a callous indifference. In diametric contrast, the pagans, free from the tyrannical rule of Iahvèh, are described as primitive people who have succeeded in dominating nature and who have learned to live in harmony with one another under the benevolent guidance of dignified elders. The antithesis makes it plain that Leconte de Lisle conceived of "Qaïn" as a bitter indictment against arbitrariness of a rule in which men will be pushed to commit crimes against their own volition. Such an indictment, of course, is deeply immersed in the poet's own metaphysical pessimism.

For the most part, Leconte de Lisle's poem displays little concern with the reconstruction of the various episodes in the biblical legend. The sequential order of events which frames this epic account provides the backdrop for Cain's lament which gives the poem its major thrust. As an interpretation of the story of Cain and Abel, the poem contains a lyrical ingredient which enables de Lisle's rendering to transcend the immediacy of any specific biblical incident in order to make a more generalized comment on the plight of man. The effectiveness of "Qaïn" rests upon the poetic and dramatic articulation of the human condition which has been bestowed on man ever since the time of Cain.

One of the most effectively lyrical sequences in the poem occurs when the seer, Thogorma, calls out to Cain in his dream. The latter awakens, and asks why he has been summoned after ten centuries of sleep. He would like to speak once again to the jealous God, and he recalls with painful nostalgia the original innocence of the earth which was permeated with a primitive and uncorrupted love of life. He evokes the Eden, terrestrial paradise, from which fate so cruelly excluded him:

Eden! What a dazzling and short-lived vision you have been for me! You, which existed before the time in which I was disinherited! Eden! Eden! Now, my frustrated heart sees the form of its dream change

[72]

abruptly, and only the sword glows in the lost horizon. Eden! The dearest and most soothing of all dreams! You, for which I have cried so uselessly! The curse of God has swept me far away from your sacred walls which remain closed to me forever. You have been plunged like a lost sun into a wavy abyss.[12]

Underscored in his evocation of a lost Eden is the fact that Cain considers his only crime to have been to desire something which a jealous Jehovah made impossible for him to attain. In other words, man is goaded by a tempting offer which is ultimately never granted by "the tormentor of the world and of living man."

In what might conceivably be interpreted as a parodistic inversion of Christ's Resurrection, Cain is made to arise from the grave and to again walk the earth which has constituted his prison. But Cain rises not to proclaim the goodness of God, but to indict him for his cruelty. When Cain encounters the sentinel, Khéroub, he is reproached by him for his persistent defiance of the will of God. The first biblical revolutionary replies proudly that he will never submit since such submission bespeaks an enslavement to God and increases his own degradation as a man. Cain's entreaty with Khéroub underscores with acute precision the nature of the former's revolt against God.

Return to your own nothingness, earthworm that you are! Of what possible use is your futile revolt against the One who can accomplish all things? The first mocks the water which murmurs and boils; the wind does not hear the lament of the dead leaf. Kneel down and pray.—I shall remain standing! Cowards may crawl under the foot of the master who subdues them. They glorify their own shame and they adore their torment since they win their rest through a debasement of themselves. Iahvèh, when he blesses them in their mire and in their shame, approves a terror which flatters and a hatred which lies to him. I shall remain standing! I shall remain standing from night until dawn and from dawn until night. I shall never stop emitting the cry of an anguished soul in despair! I am consumed by a thirst for justice, Khéroub. Crush me, for I will never submit! Let the darkness answer me! Let Iahvèh answer me! I suffer, and do not know what I have done.—The sentinel, Khéroub replies: Qaïn! Iahvèh has willed that it be so. Keep quiet, and go on your terrible way.—Dark Spirit of the night, there is an evil in the world. Tell me, why was I born?—You will know why tomorrow.—I did find out why I was born. Like the blinded bear which staggers into the trench where death has been stalking him for so long, whipped into a frenzy, drunk, deaf and bewildered, I fell into Iahvèh's unavoidable ambush, and it is he who pushed me to commit the crime for which he had created me.[13]

Leconte de Lisle found in the biblical figure of Cain a willing spokesman for many of the views and feelings which shaped the principles upon which he evolved his own philosophical pessimism. His poem is much more concerned with the examination of the motives in Cain's revolt and the nature of God's injustice toward man than it is concerned with the reconstruction of the biblical legend for its own sake. In a last speech to posterity, his Qaïn prophesies the rebirth of his spirit which shall one day manage to throw off the yoke of subjugation. At such a time, all of the men and the cities, previously destroyed by an arbitrary deity, will be resuscitated and restored as the new Eden which will witness a new Abel deriving from Cain, and which will exultantly proclaim the impotence of the Creator. In this epic poem, de Lisle conveys his strongest expression of the inevitability of evil in a world which has been so imperfectly created. Irving Putter judiciously points out that the theme of vengeance which is spelled out in "Qaïn" confers an incongruous quality to the work inasmuch as it emerges as an emotional outburst against the poet's own metaphysical outlook: "Revolt against fate may have its bitter satisfactions, but it is doomed to failure like all human efforts. Suffering and evil can never disappear until the world itself has ceased to exist." [14] Be that as it may, the sense of raucousness and harshness which "Qaïn" unleashes constitutes reason enough for it to be inserted in this collection on the Barbarian races such as de Lisle understood the term.

II   *The Jungle or Animal Poems*

There can be no dismissing the fact that for a great many readers, even today, Leconte de Lisle's most uncontested achievement as a poet rests squarely upon the series of animal or jungle evocations which made their way into the *Poèmes barbares* and later into the *Poèmes tragiques*. Such poems as "L'Oasis," "Le Rêve du jaguar," "La Panthère noire," "Les Eléphants," "Le Sommeil du condor," and "Les Hurleurs" are striking portraits of wild animals captured in characteristic poses which translate with eloquence their innate primitivism and barbarism. Con-

[74]

spicuously absent from these descriptions is any kind of sentimentality which would tend to equate smaller animals with innocence and larger beasts with unmitigated carnage. The expert
blend of detail and locale stemmed from de Lisle's perceptive
observations of the caged animals in the Parisian zoological gardens and from an intelligent assimilation of the descriptive accounts of noted French Naturalists. No less a critic than Baudelaire has termed these exotic evocations of the jungle as poetic
accomplishments of the first rank: ". . . in those poems not primarily concerned with religious ideas or the evolution of human
thought, the poet has managed to describe Beauty such as it has
manifested itself to him: the awesome, crushing forces of nature,
the dignity of animals in motion and at rest. . . . In such moments,
Leconte de Lisle emerges as a master, and a great master at
that." [15]

The fact of the matter was that, in varying degrees, each animal or jungle evocation underlined the courageous yet inexorable
struggle for existence which constitutes a major motif in his entire
poetic production.[16] Leconte de Lisle saw in animals the same
vital instinct for survival which he detected in human beings. As
far as he was concerned, the Darwinian thesis of the *Origin of
Species,* translated into French in 1862, gave scientific confirma-
tion to the pessimistic attitudes which he had adopted earlier.
At best, the animal poems are pictorial accounts of the hopelessness of the struggle. His tiger, lion, jaguar, and panther all par-
take of the same struggle for existence which justifies their sinister
carnage. In other words, there evists no higher law in the jungle
than that of kill or be killed. It is no mere coincidence that Leconte de Lisle should avoid the stereotyped images of these wild
beasts as the triumphant lords of the jungle. For all of the power
and energy which these portraits convey, it is more precisely the
sense of fearful anticipation that is dramatically unfolded. In the
end, animal life undergoes the same inexorable fate as human life.
The superiority of de Lisle's portraits over those of such counterparts as Vigny and even Baudelaire proceeds from portrayals
which are essentially steeped in primitivism. Even though he
eventually makes his jungle poems reflect in some way his own
metaphysical pessimism, he eschews the more exclusively anthropomorphic approach of his congeners in Romanticism.

Literary historian Joseph Vianey has characterized Leconte de

Lisle's animal and jungle poems as "a cycle concerning the famished creatures of the world." [17] "Les Hurleurs" emphasizes the emaciated condition of howling wild dogs in the dead of the night. Their howling translates a cry of anguish as much as a cry of hunger. The eerie setting of an antagonistic nature conspires with the predicament of the starving dogs to convey the distinct impression that suffering penetrates all of creation. Leconte de Lisle's last strophe makes that point excruciatingly clear: "I do not know exactly why, but I can still hear the howling of those dogs on the beach many years after they have disappeared. I still hear, from within the depths of a confused past, the desperate cry issuing from their savage grief." [18]

For all of the barbarity of their message, these highly pictorial accounts of the wild beasts which inhabit the jungle avoid dwelling on descriptions of carnage presumably because, as so-called objective poems, they seek to elicit no emotional response of horror or pity from the reader. Leconte de Lisle never directly portrays his savage hunters while they devour their prey nor does he describe outright the killing of smaller animals for food. What ostensibly appears to be an exception to the rule, proves to be otherwise in "Le Rêve du jaguar." The description of the jaguar's slaughter of a bellowing bull turns out but to be a dream of a weary and hungry animal. Through clever indirection, "Le Rêve du jaguar" underlines its message of horror effectively and without the involvement of the horrified reader:

In the hollow of the darkened forest into which no light penetrates, he [the jaguar] collapses, stretched out on some flat rock. With one large stroke, he polishes his paw. He blinks his golden eyes made dull by sleep, and in the illusion of all of his inert strength, as he flaps his tail and shudders his flanks, he dreams that in the middle of green plantations, he is plunging with one leap his dripping claws into the flesh of some bellowing and startled bulls. [19]

Usually, de Lisle's jungle poems convey a personal theme with far more implicitness than in "Le Rêve du jaguar." Yet, the explicit manner in which he elucidates his message in this poem does not rob it of its rich poetic dimension.

First published in the August 1, 1857 issue of the *Revue française,* "Le Sommeil du condor" is a remarkably effective evocation of man in his primitive state. The great condor reacts with alternative energy and impassivity to the struggle between the forces of light and darkness. As witness to the dramatic conflict from the perspective of the highest mountain peak of the Cordilleras ranges in the Andes, the South American bird watches impassively as the powers of the night assert their triumph over the declining light of the setting sun. Through the eyes of the solitary condor, the reader visualizes the horrifying sight of summit after summit being engulfed in the all-pervading darkness. With discernible haughtiness and impassivity, the mighty bird lets out a raucous cry, and, in a sudden burst of energy, flees the encompassing night as it soars higher toward the beckoning light of the Southern Cross. The raucous cry translates his hope of escape or deliverance from the black abyss. Far from the darkened earth below, the condor finally stops to sleep in the icy air, its great wings spread in a gesture of immobility.

What renders "Le Sommeil du condor" so memorable is the manner in which the visual and auditory devices employed heighten the poem's thematic content. The bird's raucous noise and flapping of its wing on the snow, and finally its energetic ascension into the sky—all are admirably suggested by the poet's felicitous use of the twelve-foot line in which alternating rhymes convey a lingering effect that is admirably suited to the vast expanses evoked. The condor's poetic escape from an encompassing darkness underscores a majestic grandeur which Leconte de Lisle identifies here with a primitive barbarism. The solitary position of the condor, his energetic flight toward the realization of his aspiration, and his subsequent sleep in icy immobility translate handsomely the poet's interpretation of dominant life attitudes. A prominent Parnassian concern with precision and accuracy prevents "Le Sommeil du condor" from degenerating into overbearing emotionalism. The utilization of characteristic traits in the description of the condor's predicament endows the tableau with a vivid sense of reality:

And it [the darkness] took hold of the muted continent from the sands to the slopes, from the gorges to the mountains and from summit to summit, it swells in crossing the heavy overflow of its own tide. And, like a specter, alone in front of the highest peak, bathed in the last rays of light which bleed upon the snow, he awaits the sinister sea of darkness which will overtake him. It arrives and unfurls itself as it encompasses him completely. In the endless abyss of blackness, the Southern Cross lights up the edges of the sky with its flashing constellation. His throat rattles with pleasure as he stirs up his plumage and raises his peeled, muscular neck. He rises in the air while he lashes away at the bitterly cold snow of the Andes. And with a raucous cry, he flies to the heights where the winds will be unable to reach him, and now, far from the darkened globe below and far from the living star above, he sleeps in the icy air with his splendid wings outstretched.[20]

"Les Eléphants" is Leconte de Lisle's splendid evocation of a herd of elephants traversing the desert. The animals are seen from the poet's perspective: they are at first perceived vaguely on the horizon, then they parade more closely before they disappear into the horizon. This is a vision in which realistic detail and description blend skillfully with the imaginative elements which are deployed. The setting emphasizes the silence and the solitude that envelops the desert at the moment in which the poetic vision takes place. The endless sands are likened to a sea which has been set afire by the intense heat of the sun. Except for the barely perceptive movements of a giraffe and a boa in the distance, all life in the desert appears immersed in a deep sleep. It is into such an ambience that the poet notices the herd of approaching elephants. With just a few characteristic traits, a vivid presence of the animals is evoked before they are allowed to disappear again as a black line on the distant horizon. Through the poet's imagination, the reader is able to catch a fleeting glimpse of the elephants' nostalgic longing for a primitive existence. De Lisle's poem centers around the notion that the animals are returning in pilgrimage to the land of their origin. To achieve their aim, they patiently suffer the physical discomfort of the flies which swarm about their bodies and of the scorching sun which renders their voyage across the desert sands more difficult to endure. "Les Eléphants" makes skillful use of physical description in order to convey the psychological frame of reference which the poet attributes to the animals. In this instance, a relationship is established between the evocation of the elemental instincts of the elephants and Leconte de Lisle's nostalgic yearning for the prenatal state of nonbeing.

*　　*　　*

On their march, they [the elephants] dream of the land which they have left and of the forests of fig-trees where their race took shelter. They will see the river again which fell from the great mountains and in which the enormous hippopotamus swims as he bellows, and to which, their forms whitened under the moon, they used to go and drink as they would flatten the flowering rush.[21]

III *The Love Lyrics*

For all of his official concern with objectivity and impassibility, Leconte de Lisle comes perilously to the brink of losing some of his Parnassian composure in the series of poems which may be described with accuracy as love lyrics. Unlike so many poets of his generation who fell away to a scientific or positivist penchant in which they subjected the matters of the heart to the hard and objective scrutiny of detailed analysis, he displays in the love poems a freshness and a youthful innocence that is seldom encountered in Parnassian poetry. This is not to say that de Lisle's attitude toward love is not at least partly rooted in his general philosophical outlook. Indeed, in such poems as "Ultra Coelos," for example, love is depicted as the futile expression of man's aspiration toward a state of permanence which is denied by life itself. Such a conclusion falls, of course, neatly in line with similar views propounded elsewhere and constitutes part and parcel of a fundamental theme which invests most of his work. For the most part, however, such a judgment as that elucidated in "Ultra Coelos" rarely asserts itself so directly in love verses which appear mainly preoccupied with imparting a simple impression or message that is most likely derived from the poet's personal experience.

Prior to his marriage in 1857, Leconte de Lisle experienced bitter disillusionment and dejection in the aftermath of an extended liaison with the wife of his painter friend, Jobbé-Duval. Whether his love lyrics exalt the birth and exhilaration of passion or decry the perfidy of women, most poems go to considerable lengths to avoid any direct expression of emotion. In a general way, de Lisle's love verses tend to evoke a generalized experience when they are cast in the form of ballads or legends such as in "Les Elfes," "Christine," and "Ekhidna." It is only when de Lisle abandons the screen for his own emotions that he flirts with the kind of shameless public confession that he denounces in his celebrated programmatic sonnet, "Les Montreurs." In "La Vipère," for instance, the poem's concluding vituperative bidding vies ironically enough with Musset's pelican tearing painfully at his vitals in "La Nuit de mai."

But if love's bitter venom has made its way into your veins, and if you have grown pale by a tearful pleasure and languor, know that your search for a remedy for your suffering is a vain search, for the anguish of nothingness will inundate your heart. Broken by the burden of shame and misery for such an abominable evil, do not allow your life to be consumed by it. Either tear out the mortal viper from your bosom or keep quiet, you coward, and die. Yes, let yourself die for having loved too completely.[22]

The conjuration of love as a torture for man is conveyed in such poems as "Le Dernier Souvenir," "La Mort du soleil," and "Les Spectres" in a less directly emotional manner than in "La Vipère." Much like his Romantic counterpart, Alfred de Vigny, Leconte de Lisle, more frequently than not, sought to temper his personal response to experience by resorting to symbols which endowed his verse with at least the apparent air of objectivity.

Leconte de Lisle betrays, as much by the nature of his legendary sources and by his adaptations of them, at least a partial disposition toward a treatment of the theme of love that was most in conformity with his pessimistic assessment of human existence. The poem, "Christine," which first appeared in the *Poèmes et poésies* of 1855, is a case in point. As Xavier Marmier relates this Scandinavian legend in his *Chants populaires du nord,* Christine is portrayed in her bereavement for her fiancé who has died. One night, he comes to her door, speaks to her, and sleeps with her until the dawn signals his return to the cemetery where he has been entombed. Beside herself with grief, Christine vows to remain seated on her lover's tomb until her own death. But the voice of the fiancé entreats her to cease weeping and to leave since each tear inundates his grave with blood. He requests that in the name of their love, she assume an air of gaiety since her smiles fill his tomb with roses. Leconte de Lisle's alteration of the poem's ending approximates more closely the attitude which dominates most of the *Poèmes barbares:*

*   *   *

And when they had arrived under the black pine trees of the cemetery, he spoke to her: —Good bye! I only beseech that you leave me now, my beloved, and that you continue to live! —But as she joined her hand in his, she descended first into the tomb. Thus, ever since that day, the two of them sleep in the same tomb under the bronze cross. Oh! for the divine sleep which intoxicates the mind! They are able to love for all time. Happy are those who can live and die as they did.[23]

The short allegorical poem, "Le Colibri," which celebrates the ecstasy of the first kiss, translates the almost inescapable conclusion that Leconte de Lisle's love lyrics underscore, in varying degrees, all that which he would have liked to find in the passion.[24]

IV   *The Nature Poems*

Leconte de Lisle's pessimism stemmed from his acute consciousness that man's desire for the absolute remained indubitably contradicted by the limitation imposed by a finite, material existence. His acceptance of a religious relativism, resulting from a seemingly more objective approach to metaphysical problems, prevented him, in the long run, from founding his own lyrical impulse on any personally evolved transcendentalism. Unlike such Romantic counterparts as Lamartine, who saw in nature the direct reflection of a future state of being, he tended to view nature as a recollective depository for all human aspiration and experience. De Lisle's nature poems are rooted in an explicit nostalgia for the past of his youth. The inclusion of poems such as "La Fontaine aux lianes," "Le Manchy," "Le Bernica," and "La Ravine Saint-Gilles" in a collection like the *Poèmes barbares* is justified by their generous reference to the luxuriance of a primitive nature. By and large, these poems remove us from all of the busy preoccupations of sophisticated, pragmatic societies and absorb us in the exoticism of a still primitive land. Such exoticism, of course, serves as a temporary refuge for the poet's metaphysical anguish. The very titles of de Lisle's poems evoke the exoticism of some tropical island—most likely his native Réunion—but a close reading of these verses reveals that their settings are situated as much in the poet's imagination as in any particular place.

Probably the most famous of Leconte de Lisle's nature poems, "Le Manchy" is considerably more than the simple evocation of a beautiful young girl being brought to Sunday church services on a palanquin borne by slaves. "Le Manchy" is a highly visual celebration of a way of life which is permeated with a sense of primitive grandeur. The young Creole lady is portrayed in the background of an indolently warm yet radiantly fresh tropical environment. Much has been offered by way of explanation concerning the nature of the relationship between the poet and Elixenne de Lanux, whose likeness is evoked in "Le Manchy." But such matters of personal background need not deter us from responding to the poem on its own aesthetic and emotional merits. The allusions to the young Creole's jewelry, her costume, the perfumed vegetation, the exotic musical instruments played by a mixture of the island's races, and the *manchy* itself: all of these elements conspire to conjure up more than the simple etching of a single person as she is being carried to church on any given Sunday morning. What "Le Manchy" actually evokes is the vision of the composite ideal woman, whose physical and spiritual embodiment is a product of the poet's creative imagination. Because Leconte de Lisle is recalling an incident which occurred in the somewhat distant past, he has managed, in the poem, to establish an aesthetic distance between himself and the object of his contemplation. The portrait is conspicuously lacking in all coy sentimentality. Rather, a certain momentary fusion of time and place endows this nostalgic poem with the illusion that such a felicitous experience may be crystallized into some form of permanence. The concluding stanza of "Le Manchy," however, recalls the reader to a more delimiting reality as the nostalgic reverie turns to the present tense.

And as a butterfly with its open azure-blue and scarlet wings would rest on your delicate skin, leaving on it a small imprint of its colors, one could see through the cambric curtain golden curls which were unfurled on the pillow. And beneath those half-closed lids, one could see your somberly beautiful amethyst eyes as you pretended to sleep. Thus, you would come to high mass from the mountains on those exceedingly mild mornings in the rosy freshness of your youth and in your simple grace to the rhythmic footsteps of your Hindu servants. Today, you are at rest among the dead who are dear to me, in the arid sands of our shores under the couch-grass. All that remains is the noise from the sea. You, the delectable charm of my first aspirations! [25]

*   *   *

"La Fontaine aux lianes" recalls Baudelaire's "La Vie antérieure" by its simply stated nostalgia for the prenatal state of man. Leconte de Lisle recasts the past that he evokes through the perspective of his later experiences. To an extent, the nature that he recalls issues from both his imagination and his sense of observation. In "La Fontaine aux lianes," the recollection of the natural setting of the Réunion that he knew as a young man reawakens in him the desire to return to the original state of being which he imagines to be untroubled by the pain and anguish caused by the desire of self-fulfillment. The poem illustrates what the poet meant when he defined lyricism as the formal expression which serves as an intermediary between the idea of lasting beauty and the senses through which we receive intimations of such permanence:

There was once a spring tide in which the waters seemed still, deep in the forests which were bathed in a celestial vapor. Only a few sweet rushes, guardians of the rustic fountain, leaned over the water as if in silent witness. The huge water lilies and the creeping liana, like white archipelagos, crisscrossed one another in the water whose transparent profundity catches the reflection of another sky where birds swim. Oh! coolness of the forests, man's first serenity! Oh! winds which caress the murmuring leaves, and fountains whose ripples play with the sunlight! Eden, extended to the green eminences, I greet you! I greet you also, gentle peace! And you, pure breaths which come directly from the heavens and the reeds, you are the refuge of my heart, and the haven of forgetfulness of my joys and sorrows! I greet you, oh! sanctuary from which all human suffering is excluded! [26]

Leconte de Lisle's conception of nature, such as it becomes manifest in "La Fontaine aux lianes," differs substantively from the usual Romantic interpretation in which nature is seen as a kind of material trampoline upon which the thoughts of men spring forth toward notions of the infinite and the eternal. In "La Fontaine aux lianes," nature becomes a refuge where men attempt to blunt the acuteness of the consciousness of their predicament. The landscape bespeaks a stillness which contrasts dramatically with the enervating movement associated with modern civilizations. In a sense, the poem is a celebration of the type of immobility, only found in primitive ambiences, which allows men to bask momentarily in the illusion that all desire and aspiration is absorbed in a quiet peace and contentment. Such a state of being resides, of course, in the poet's own imagination and in the power of his recollection. "Le Bernica" resembles in many ways "La Fontaine aux lianes' insomuch as the stillness that is evoked is associated with the mountain refuge recalled by Leconte de Lisle.

Technically, "La Vérandah" reveals the poet's clever handling of the envelope motif to convey a theme that is somewhat allied to that of "La Fontaine aux lianes." The atmosphere that is conjured up is one of near-absolute silence. The only detectable movement is the slight breeze which subtly embalms the nature setting with the sweet perfume of the jasmines. The disposition of the rhymes and the imagery simulates a gently monotonous refrain that lulls and soothes the senses. The opening and closing of each of the seven-line strophes repeat the same motif. The effect achieved is that of an ecstatic feeling for the void that is entombed in archaic stillness. Everything in "La Vérandah" leads up to the final affirmation in the closing lines of the last strophe: "Everything is reduced to silence. The slender bird and the jealous hornet stop their quarreling around the ripe fig trees, and the rose trees of Iran have stopped their murmuring. The spring tide drops off to sleep in the middle of its red-brown porphyry." [27]

However attenuated in mood and tone the so-called nature poems may apear to us by comparison with more direct expressions of despair and disillusionment, it would be a gross exaggeration to conclude that Leconte de Lisle found in nature a wholly satisfactory resolution of his dilemma. "Ultra Coelos" underscores with almost painful explicitness that nature is but the crucible in which man attempts unsuccessfully to deaden the excruciating desire toward an impossible objective. Central to the poet's philosophical pessmism is the realization that such desire can never be fully assuaged. Nature is capable of lulling man in a temporary illusion that the answer to his aspiration lies within its bosom. But the tragic human dilemma rests ultimately upon the unshakable premise that desire is goaded by a permanence which resides beyond the illusory permanence of a nature which apparently renews itself in endless fashion. What such poems as "La Fontaine aux lianes" and "Le Vérandah" leave implicit, "Ultra Coelos" spells out in unmistakable language: let us make the most of this human torment by living since we are unable either to forget our plight or to die.

But, alas! Oh, Nature! It is not you whom we love, since you do not cause us to cry or to bleed. You appear oblivious to our cries of love and anathema, and you do not seem moved by the fact that you dazzle us. Your chalice, which is always filled, is pressed too close to our lips. It is the bitter cup of desire that we need! A fatal clarion rings out in our fever and says: Arise and walk, run, fly, farther, higher! Oh wandering larva which whirls round and round in count-less swarms, do not ever stop! With bloodied feet, climb the golden steps of the world. And, hearts which overflow with sobs, beat in other breasts! No, it was never you, infinite solitude, whose inexpressi-ble concerts I used to listen to! Rather, it was he who whipped up a bitter harmony in the brain of a dreamy child outstretched on the deserted sands of the beach.[28]

V *The Middle Ages*

The cycle of poems underscoring the Barbarism of the Middle Ages comes closest to revealing what we might term a virtual abandonment of Leconte de Lisle's vaunted pose of objectivity and impassibility in the *Poèmes barbares.* The poet's contempt for the period in which Christianity flourished asserts itself with categorical force in poems such as "La Vision de Snorr," "Un Acte de charité," and "Les Paraboles de Dom Guy." Personally revulsed by the Church's active collaboration with the regime of Louis-Napoleon during the 1850's and 1860's, he tended to view Catholicism primarily as a powerful temporal force whose wanton political role betrayed in the most outrageous fashion the very spirit of its founder. The poems on the Middle Ages and on Chris-tianity denounce the highly ritualized character of a faith which has seemingly become devoid of all genuine spiritual meaning. "La Vision de Snorr" and "Un Acte de charité" disclose the kind of fanaticism wrought by a religious organization bent on the absolute subjugation of its members and adherents. De Lisle's poems underline his opinion that Christianity, like the religions before it, has outlived its usefulness to man as a meaningful guide. What is clearly displayed in these verses, which evoke a barbaric cruelty and ignorance, is the view that Christianity is little more than an elaborate caste which preaches messages antithetical to those of Christ. By its insistence upon the afterlife of which it possesses no real knowledge, Christianity intensifies the anguish residing in man's predicament since it requests that he abandon the present for some future whose existence cannot be ascertained. In modern times, then, Christianity becomes the pernicious agent of man's moral decadence. Leconte de Lisle's cycle on the Middle Ages evolves from the conclusions inspired by such an optic or frame of reference.

"La Vision de Snorr" owes its primary inspiration to the thirteenth-century account of an Icelandic priest's vision of hell, whose transcription was used to persuade untutored peasants to embrace Christianity. Leconte de Lisle is, of course, hardly interested in Sömund's account as a religious or as an historical document. Sömund's account of the vision, such as it was incorporated in *Les Chants de Sôl*, constitutes in itself a fascinating portrait of the Icelandic conception of hell. De Lisle renders the Islandic version even more horrifying by dwelling on the huge inventory of tortures endured by the victims who have been thrust into hell. To a great extent, "La Vision de Snorr" is a satirical commentary on the manner in which various types of rabid fanaticism interpret the forces of good and evil. The nineteenth-century interpretation of Snorr's vision of the eternal fires emphasizes the hallucinatory aspects contained in the Icelandic priest's narrative, and expands on the kinds of cruel and barbaric punishment that is dispensed to the damned. The poet displays his complete exasperation with Christianity in the closing stanzas of "La Vision de Snorr," which depict the horrible tortures that are held in reserve for those who have not been enlightened by its message:

Finally, I can see the blind and stupid people who lived in Ancient times, the race which lived before the advent of your light, Lord!, and which made its way, alas, without ever really knowing where it was going. They are like a huge whirlwind of living dust which a false wind pushes on in any haphazard fashion. Their brows are dazzled only by the light of the Devil's sun. But, you have certainly favored us, and our only complaint is that we still remain on this iniquitous earth. You came too late for the Ancients, though. Thus, everyone wears on his forehead a Runic letter which transforms his brain into a smoldering brand. After all, they remained ignorant of the law of your only Son. And so, torture upon torture, pain after pain, harnessed

in burning iron collars, and dressed in cloaks of fire, they endure all of
that for all time! [29]

   As Leconte de Lisle comes nearer to his own epoch, he abandons legend and myth for historical anecdotes as the source of his
inspiration. His aversion for the Middle Ages scarcely remained
a secret locked in his soul; he asserted his outright contempt for
that period of history in his acceptance discourse at the French
Academy: ". . . the Middle Ages are a blot in history. These were
years filled with the kind of abominable barbarity which led to
the virtual extinction of the cultural wealth bequeathed by Antiquity, and which contaminated the human mind by repeated
outbreaks of the most inept superstitions and of the bloody
tyranny of religious fanaticism." [30] "Un Acte de charité" captures
much of Leconte de Lisle's contemptuous regard for Christianity.
The poem expresses the horror which the poet experiences before
wanton acts of cruelty perpetrated in Christ's name. "Un Acte de
charité" recounts the despair which overtook a noble lady when
she realized that all of her alms giving had barely attenuated the
suffering of the starving masses. After assembling her six hundred
mendicants in a barn, she proceeded to set a torch to it from the
outside, convinced that her act constituted the will of God. The
last two stanzas convey the poet's unmistakable reaction.

Crying bitterly, she lit the fire at the various angles of the pine and
thatched nook:—I have done all that I could, and I now commend
your spirits to God. May Jesus welcome you in his kingdom!—Thus,
they all entered into their eternity. A quick death is followed by a
welcome peace. As for the Lady, she lived the remainder of her life
in a cloister. May God in his infallible equity judge her! [31]

   Recalling the France of the 1400's, "Les Paraboles de Dom
Guy" is a somewhat overlong and frequently overbearing inventory of the various sins and crimes committed allegedly by the
Medieval clergy. Leconte de Lisle paints a most loathsome pic-
ture of the Middle Ages in language that is so categorical as to
betray a personal obsession and prejudice. Clearly, he can associate no good with the entire period. Anatole France, himself no
fervent defender of organized Christianity, was prompted to
make the following judgment on de Lisle's series: "He only sees

famines, leprosy, ignorance and burning stakes. In point of fact, there are other things in the Middle Ages. . . . M. Leconte de Lisle portrays a period of history that has elicited his hatred, And like the hatred of poets, it is a very great and simple hatred." [32] Such outright contempt and disdain for the Medievalism which became so prominently identified with Christianity predicted the highly vituperative tone assumed in the pamphlet which he published in 1871, *Histoire populaire du Christianisme*. Much of the exaggeration and the uncontrolled personal bias which are detectable in such poems as "La Vision de Snorr" and "Les Paraboles de Dom Guy" are in no small way attributable to a certain carelessness with formal precision. Leconte de Lisle has allowed his own emotional response to interfere with an objectified presentation of the issues in question. There can be no doubt that such personal outbursts have affected negatively the artistic integrity of the poet in such instances. The tighter technical control in evidence in "Le Nazaréen" achieves the poet's artistic objective with considerably more success.

Attached to the cycle of poems on the Middle Ages, more for its thematic content than for any specific historical association with Medievalism, "Le Nazaréen" is an elaboration of the question of Christ's doubt and despair as found in *Matthew* 27: 46–50, "Le Nazaréen" focuses on Christ's lament as his body is being nailed to the cross. The complaint voiced is one reverberated by all of humanity: religious principle, however firmly established, succumbs in the end to the relativism of time. The lyricism of this poem is touching in its own right, and the pessimism which is undeniably dispelled is framed in a general commentary on man's predicament. Contained within this larger and more meaningful context, Leconte de Lisle's criticism of Christianity does not detract from the poem's thematic unity. Indeed, such comments are clearly subordinated to the principal theme. The shorter form of "Le Nazaréen"—twelve four-line stanzas—serves as a disciplining factor which prevents the poet from overcharging his poem ultimately with any distracting emotionalism. The concluding four stanzas reveal the poet's technical and thematic mastery of the subject:

For you did not lie! Your Church and your glory, redeemer, can go down with the moving waves of time, and man can discard your memory without a quiver as the ashes are scattered to the four winds. On the debris of the holy cathedrals, you can hear and see the flock, livid and with flowers encircled on its forehead, fling itself at the crazy Saturnalia as its laughter insults your divine sorrow! For, now, you are seated with your Ancient Equals, and under your reddish hair, in your pure blue heaven, souls like swarms of mystical doves come to drink the dewdrops that fall from your godly lips. And, as in those proud days of the Roman apogee, just as in the decline of a blinded and revolutionary century, you shall not have lied so long as the human race bewails throughout time and eternity.[33]

VI *Modernism*

For all of their apparent harshness, the poems concerned with a barbarism which is associated with ancient tribes, Nordic traditions, wild animals, or a primeval vegetation convey in varying degrees elements of grandeur and energy which are meant to elicit our open admiration. The barbarism which Leconte de Lisle identifies with Modernism, however, is so vile and contemptible in all of its facets that it can only bestir in us a revulsion for our own epoch. Poems such as "L'Anathème," "Aux Modernes," and "Les Montreurs" make it clear that nineteenth-century man, in the poet's estimation, has managed to destroy in systematic fashion all worthwhile spiritual and intellectual values as well as natural and artistic beauty in his blind and rapacious greed for power and material luxury. "L'Anathème," in its concluding strophes, poses the hypothetical question to which the lyricist answers negatively: can man's dormant passion for freedom, justice, and beauty be revived sufficiently to bring about a civilization that is steeped in a primal force and spontaneity?

Awake and loosen your chained-up forces; let the sap run through our dried-up furrows, and let the unexpected sword gleam under blooms of myrtle as in the ancient Athenian festivals! And if you do not, and remain but an exhausted earth which is incapable of nourishing man's hope of the infinite, then, die! Do not prolong your silent agony. Return to sleep in the diluvial waves. And you, man, who still lies under the manure of the ages, you, the inheritor of men and of accrued evil, with your globe dead and your gods gone, fly away with the vile dust. Let the wild winds carry you off! [34]

First published in the June 30, 1862, issue of the *Revue contemporaine* in reply to critics concerning his so-called Parnassian impassibility, "Les Montreurs" made plain Leconte de Lisle's contemptuous regard for the majority of the writers and the general reading public of his time. Cast in the form of an allegory, the sonnet conveys the poet's innate scorn for the masses, the new barbarians, who require that authors confess their personal lives so openly in order to appease a morbid and idle curiosity. Such unabashed avowals by poets constitute no less than a prostitution of art. "Les Montreurs" likens the writer who reveals the intimacy of his existence to his audience to the chained animal who stupidly parades his enslavement for the low entertainment of a vulgar public. Through clever indirection, the sonnet articulates in succint language the Parnassian objective of a less effusive and more tightly controlled lyricism. The closing tercets are a devastating commentary on the cheapness of excessive Romantic effusion:

Even if it meant burying myself in some eternal anonymity, in my stoical pride and from the depths of my unknown grave, I would not sell the secret of my ecstasy or of my disillusionment to you [the reading public]. I refuse to expose my private life to the cries and the clamor of the general public. And I will not dance on your indiscriminate stage with your clowns and your prostitutes.[35]

"Aux Modernes" underlined the poet's acknowledged partiality for the static or dead civilizations of the past over the nineteenth century. There can be no doubting that the moderns he depicts in this sonnet represent the most repulsive barbarian types which are evoked in the entire collection. For all of its violent invective against contemporary mores, "Les Montreurs" displays unusual containment. Leconte de Lisle's choice of such a restricted form for his most vitriolic denunciation of Modernism was a felicitous one since it required that he fuse the purely emotional elements of his inspiration with technical concision. "Les Montreurs" is a skillful condensation of a theme which could understandably have been expanded to a thousand or more lines. But much of the sonnet's effectiveness stems directly from the commentary's pungency. The visual images to which the poet has recourse appeal immediately to the imagination in these verses which decry with such vehemence the vacuity of modern man's conception of existence. De Lisle's prediction of the likely consequences

[90]

to be derived from such an empty utilitarianism points with perti-
nence to some of the problems which beset our actual societies
in the twentieth century.

You live stupid lives devoid of all dreams and worthwhile design. You
are older and even more decrepit than the barren land since you have
been cut off since your birth by the murderous century of all vigorous and profound passion. Your brain is as empty as your bosom. You
have polluted this wretched world with blood so depraved and with
a climate so foul that only death germinates from such unmentionable
mire. Men, as killers of gods, the time is fast approaching when,
stretched atop of huge heaps of gold that have been thrust in some
corner after you have finished corroding even the rocks of the earth,
you will no longer know what to do with your days and nights.
Drowning in the void of a colossal boredom, you will die stupidly as
you pointlessly stuff your pockets.[36]

The overpowering feeling which permeates the *Poèmes barbares* is one of bitter pessimism. The various cycles of the collection describe man's reaction to the hopeless enigma of his
predicament through the perspective of history. Despite an open
admiration for those examples of human dignity that are demon-
strated in the barbaric primitivism of the races which succeeded
Greek and Indian Antiquity, Leconte de Lisle shows little inclination of any kind toward a stoic resignation to fate. Unlike his
friend, Louis Ménard, who evolved a philosophy of active stoical
acceptance, Leconte de Lisle refused to elaborate any systematic
approach to life from which he could entertain, however momentarily, some kind of relative justification for human existence.
His attitude remains that of the artist who cannot substitute his
dream of the ideal by any kind of actual or relative value. Irving
Putter has described his position aptly: "An intractable idealist
imperiously governed by the need for eternity, absolute justice,
and happiness, Leconte de Lisle is unable to settle on a practical
morality." [37] As the closing poem for the *Poèmes barbares*, "Solvet
seclum" parallels, thematically, "Dies irae" which conferred a
particular finality upon the *Poèmes antiques*. "Solvet seclum"
confirms the poet's pessimism concerning man's hopeless degen-
erative descent through the ages. Deriving its inspiration from
the words of the funeral hymn inserted into the mass for the dead
in the thirteenth century, the poem conveys a quasi-hallucinatory

vision of the end of the world. The harshness of the fate awaiting man is approximated auditorily by the rasping sounds of the poem's rhythm. Whatever effect is achieved in "Solvet seclum" depends largely upon harsh sounds and images to evoke a world engulfed into nothingness.

The end of the world will occur when the globe and all of its inhabitants will be pulled out of its huge orbit like a large sterile block. Stupid, blind, and with one last howl, the earth will grow heavier and directionless, and will finally catapult itself against some motionless sphere in its blind force which will cause its wretched shell to splinter.[38]

Reaction to the *Poèmes barbares* in 1872 is somewhat crystallized by the refusal of the prestigious *Revue des deux mondes* to review the collection. Leconte de Lisle's reputation as a poet blossomed only in the early 1880's as the recognized leader of the Parnassian school of poetry. Up until that time, his verse was read by only a small minority of readers whose predispositions inspired them to look beyond the literary mainstream of the 1870's.

CHAPTER 5

The Poèmes tragiques

THE thirty-eight poems which comprise the *Poèmes tragiques* of 1884 complicate Leconte de Lisle's conception of man's ultimate absorption into nothingness with an interpretation of Darwinian transformism which coincides with his own pessimistic outlook. Whatever else, the conclusions of Darwin and Spencer, concerning the inevitable laws of survival governing both human and animal life, provided the poet who entertained a more intuitive appreciation of nature with precisely the kind of scientific verification that he sought. As the title of the collection suggests, the *Poèmes tragiques* underscores the cruelty and suffering which are endured by necessity in a world in which the struggle for life asserts itself with such unrelenting urgency. The majority of the poems in the volume describe the links that associate the predicament of man with the fate of animals. Conspicuously absent from the *Poèmes tragiques* are the verses which celebrated the quasi-superhuman traits of certain heroic types of men encountered previously in the *Poèmes antiques* and the *Poèmes barbares*. An almost entirely unrelieved emphasis on the horrible and violent aspects of existence fashions the composite image of a world singularly devoid of the kind of peace and tranquility which was so ardently desired by the poet. In a seeming effort to counterbalance the negativism residing in his abject pessimism, Leconte de Lisle displays in the *Poèmes tragiques* considerable preoccupation with purely formal and technical innovations. The inclusion of his devastating personal conclusions within the elegant formal confinement of the difficult Malaysian pantoum, for example, illustrates a discernible effort to check the extremism of his reaction within an exterior cloak of objectivity.

For the sake of convenience, we classify the verse of the *Poèmes tragiques* as fitting into one of four cycles or categories; namely, the militant poems, the historical poems, the animal poems, and the nature evocations. Directly or indirectly, and in varying degrees of intensity, the *Poèmes tragiques* betrays Leconte de Lisle's thesis concerning the desirability of the final annihilation of the human personality for want of some kind of permanent value in the universe. Just as the overwhelming number of lyrics in the *Poèmes barbares* purported to describe man's inevitable descent into degeneracy, the *Poèmes tragiques* undertook to explain that the descent of man had begun to assume a tragic character ever since Christianity's ascendancy in the Middle Ages. If the preceeding collections suggested such conclusions, this latest collection of poems portrayed the ignominy of man's fate in even more despairingly categorical terms.

I *The Militant Poems*

No single group of poems in Leconte de Lisle's entire production comes so close to a loss of control emotionally and historically as the so-called militant or anti-Catholic poems. In the poet's estimation, man's debilitated nature became the object of callous perversion by the Christian Church of the Middle Ages. It is because of the Church's perverted institutional nature that he condemns it in such sustained categorical language. "Les Siècles maudits" translates the absolute character of his condemnation of Christianity. The tone of the poem is one of near hallucination in which the Church is likened to a rapacious vampire.

Centuries of aspergillums, cowls, and penitents' hoods, of strappados and trestles from which the Roman ghoul, this vampire, drunk on human blood, frothing with enraged teeth, and with a torch in his hand, brandishes the flesh of all living souls with the anguish of being alive in the world and with the terror of death as he consecrates to the stupid fires of Hell a smoldering holocaust on the iron-clad altar! For each one of the despicable minutes of your existence, oh! centuries [Middle Ages] of stranglers, cowards and unspeakable brutes, you are the shame of this old globe and of humanity. May you be damned, and damned for all eternity! [1]

Presumably derived from the *Apocalypse* and somewhat inspired by Vigny's "Le Mont des Oliviers," "La Bête écarlate" conveys with greater accuracy Leconte de Lisle's distinction between religious feeling and religious form.[2] The poem evokes the tragic figure of Jesus as he meditates the night of his betrayal. In a moment of vision, he witnesses his followers, the Christians, who discard his message of universal love and charity for selfish and stupid concern with theories of personalized eternal happiness. He retreats in horror at the tortures and crimes of their invention. Rising in disgust and in contempt at the Apocalyptic beast which personifies his Church, he despairs of mankind and embraces his own death as a deliverance. "La Béte écarlate" pits Jesus against Christianity, and confirms the fact that Leconte de Lisle's attack upon religion is principally upon its aggressive institutionality which, in his view, has vitiated the doctrine of love of its founder. The concluding section of "La Bête écarlate" makes this point most effectively:

And when the Man awakened from his dream, he was silent, gasping, and livid. His whole body perspired with anguish and disgust before the sight of this horrible hell which he had witnessed, with its wave of blood and hatred, its centuries of pain and its peoples subjugated like animals, and this Scarlet Monster and these demons which all roared his name! This was the real eternity of tortures! And, falling to the ground as he heaved a huge sigh, the Man despaired of the world and wished for his death.[3]

What distinguishes "La Bête écarlate" from Vigny's "Le Mont des Oliviers," which treats a similar theme, is de Lisle's method of presentation. Whereas Vigny relied almost exclusively on the interplay between images of light and darkness to convey his point, "La Bête écarlate" juxtaposes images of human behavior with animal behavior to suggest the ultimate assimilation of the former by the latter. The final impression emerging from the visionary account is that of the reduction of man to the status of a beast, a condition which becomes further aggravated by the aggressive intrusion of an absurd Christendom. The poet expresses feelings in this poem which are virtually of the same intensity as those encountered in the more vitriolic "Les Siècles maudits," but the violent interjection of emotion is avoided, for the most part, because the poet's reactions are expressed only indirectly through the intermediary of the visionary account. The effect achieved in "La Bête écarlate" is a significantly more felicitous one than "Les Siècles maudits." By so camouflaging his own feelings, Leconte de Lisle conveys with more clarity and objectivity what he considers to be the scandalous disparity between the spirit of the Catholic Church and the spirit bequeathed it by its founder. Such a view informs all of his criticism of the Christian Middle Ages.

"Le Lévrier de Magnus" is a long narrative poem which recounts the mysterious return of the Duke of Magnus to his castle on the Rhine some sixty years after his departure on a Crusade against the Turks of the Holy Land. The entire first section of the poem succeeds marvelously in evoking the sense of an impending doom by its insistence on such eerie imagery as the intent stare of the large, emaciated black deerhound, the specter of three mute Saracens, and a raucous howling of the wind which envelops the duke's cavernous castle. The description of the fearful and superstitious peasants who dare not approach the forbidding setting cleverly implies that what will be related in the three subsequent sections of "Le Lévrier de Magnus" is rooted in myth and legend. The second section is a rapid survey of a Christian Crusade during the Middle Ages seen through the perspective of the German knight, Magnus, who, in retrospect, shrinks back emotionally from the rape and pillage committed in the name of Christianity. The lone survivor of a bloody battle against the Turks, Magnus betrayed his honor and his pledge in exchange for all the luxury and comfort which he had always secretly coveted:

Let him delight in all that of which he has dreamed, of riches during the day and of sensual pleasure at night. And may Mahomet welcome him in his joyous Sabbaths! For he is young and brave and strong, and who knows how many such triumphant days he has left? And once all of his desires shall have been fully realized, he will repent in the decline of his life. Aren't more rapacious clerics and more contemptible monks, in fact, absolved without the hint of scandal upon payment of a few pieces of gold? And, if need be, he will pledge to the Holy See his feudal lands and the black vermiculated dungeon where the bones of his ancestors grow white under the marble slabs.[4]

The third part of "Le Lévier de Magnus" underscores the depravity of the Lombardian duke who is depicted as leading an attack upon a Carmelite convent which had enjoyed the protection of a recently deceased Saracen leader. The nuns are defiled by the soldiers, and Magnus brutally rapes the abbess, Alix. Be-

lieving herself to be excluded from heaven because of her tainted
virginity, Alix kills herself as she vows to haunt Magnus for the
remainder of his life. So that her soul might be purified, the
spirit of Alix is made to occupy the form of a black deerhound
which remains at the constant side of Magnus. The fourth section
of the poem makes a complete circle with the first part. Haunted
perpetually by the memory of his awful crime by the presence of
the dog and the specter of the three mute Saracens, Magnus is
finally driven to engulf himself in the fiery abyss of death. His
dying words, however, are those of defiance, and they recall to
some extent the deprecations of the beleaguered Kaïn in the
Poèmes barbares:

Magnus! Magnus! the all-devouring fire awaits you, and the opal is
flowing around your finger which it inflames. Just repent, and you
can avoid this irrevocable journey.—No! I shall not ask God for his
forgiveness! Has He not made my soul the way it is so that it is capable
of breaking without giving way? If He has made me thus, then, let
Him assume the responsibility for my crime! [5]

The decidedly Darwinian motif in Magnus's final speech as well
as Alix's transformation into an animal underlines Leconte de
Lisle's likening of man's fate to that of animals. The poet's criticism of the Medieval Crusades is subordinated to such a consid-
eration in "Le Lévrier de Magnus."

The idea of the cruelly repressive nature of organized Christianity as well as its aggressive opposition to art and beauty is
brought forth in "L'Holocauste" which narrates the fiery martyr-
dom that a seventeenth-century atheist suffered at the hands
of a motley group of Catholic tormentors. "L'Holocauste" virtually abounds in disgusting images which are drawn expressly
to elicit the reader's response of horror before the atrocity that
is perpetrated in the name of Christ. Leconte de Lisle juxtaposes
two viewpoints in the poem—that of the martyr and that of the
crowd which attends the execution—to underscore all the more
dramatically the demeaning character of an institution which
demonstrates blatant disregard for life and beauty. The evocation
of the crowd that has come to watch with glee the burning of a
human life at the stake conjures up an atmosphere of ugliness and
animalistic brutality:

And as the masses swirl about, stumble and kick in the confusion, their eyes are wide-open and their arms are up in the air. The crowd is made up of monks in white, grey and brown habits, some wearing long beards, others, close-shaven. Some are washed and others are unwashed, and there are men in capes, frocks and in penitent's hoods. Old women grate their teeth like ghouls, and cavaliers are there also, plumed and feather-legged. Some rogues are cutting capers on the sharp-pointed paving-stone while ladies in stiff skirts remain seated in carriages or on chairs. There are also fat townsmen that are bloated with the redness of good wines imprinted on their cheeks, along with bullies and old soldiers in the jumbled herd of boors, tramps and prostitutes.[6]

Leconte de Lisle's sustained bitterness with respect to organized religion in the militant poems is doubtless instigated by the Church's active collaboration with the Second Empire, a regime which he held accountable for the hopeless degeneracy into which modern France had fallen. Thus, the Church's most recent alliance with the forces of the new pragmatism confirmed his view that ever since its inception organized Christianity exercised but a destructive influence upon man.

II *The Historical Poems*

Poems such as "La Tête de Kenwarc'h" and "La Romance de doña Blanca," both immersed in the legendary past, made it plain that Leconte de Lisle had elected to complicate his conception of energy and heroism with a stronger influence of Darwinism in the *Poèmes tragiques*. The lengths to which he went in order to create an atmosphere of unrelieved harshness and brutality in "La Tête de Kenwarc'h: chant de mort gallois du VIe siècle" point out the fact that he sought to equate heroism in this gruesome tale with unbridled animalism. Inspired by one of Owen Jones's *Chants populaires de la Bretagne, poèmes des bardes bretons du VIe siècle* which was published in 1801, "La Tête de Kenwarc'h" recounts in somewhat drastically revised fashion the assassination of the Breton chief, Urien, by one of his soldiers as he led a battle against the Anglo-Saxons. The poem, translated into modern French by Hersart de Villemarqué, goes on to describe how Urien's head was found by a bard who sang the praises of his fallen leader and who vowed vengeance. Leconte de Lisle's version is only concerned with part of the original

poem: the most barbaric part which recalls how the chieftain's
head was carried on a spear. The poet of the *Poèmes tragiques*
changes the name of Urien to that of Kenwarc'h because of its
harsher, more Gallic sound. Much more revealing is de Lisle's
utilization of only the most brutal images that are included in
the original version.[7] The only law made manifest in "La Tête
de Kenwarc'h" is the one evoked by the behavior of wild jungle
animals: kill or be killed. Listen to the song of war of the bard-
turned-warrior:

Oc'h! The raven is joyous as it pecks at his white throat. As for me, I
proudly carry Kenwarc'h's head and its once burning eyes. In heavy
flakes just like the mousse of barley, a froth mixed with blood filters
through his teeth. Look at this head grown pale and its once burning
eyes! I shall never again hear the heroic head command and yell
under its reddish-gold torque. But I shall hoist it on the blade of my
pickaxe, and it will lead me into the thick of battle. Oc'h! Oc'h! The
Saxons will hear his battle cry! For, Kenwarc'h, your head will lead me
straight to the coward who made a hole in your back at the Cape of
Penn'hor. I will break his neck with the hammer-edge of my axe, and
I will devour his heart while it is still alive. Kenwarc'h! Oh! Wolf of
Kambrie! Oh! Cape of Penn'hor! [8]

"La Tête de Kenwarc'h" evokes the portrait of a human being
with instincts and impulses that are scarcely more evolved than
those of the animal. The bard in the poem appears to be led by
the same animalistic force that is predicated upon the sole law
of survival. Leconte de Lisle conveys the notion of a primeval
force with a categorical harshness that was absent from such
evocations in the *Poèmes antiques* and the *Poèmes barbares*. As
in other historical poems of this cycle, "La Tête de Kenwarc'h"
likens the cruelty and violence of men to those of the jungle
beasts.

III *The Animal Poems*

Whether taken individually or studied compositely, the poems
which constitute this cycle summarize most forcefully the attitudes that dominate the *Poèmes tragiques*. The poems which
translate the basic fears and hungers of the animals underline
with marvelous indirection Leconte de Lisle's pessimistic interpretation of Darwinism. In varying degrees of intensity, such

verse as that found in "Sacra fames," "L'Albatros," and "L'Incantation du loup" converges around the notion that evil and suffering are the natural by-products of all ill-constructed universe. When the idea of man's predicament is joined to the attitudes that are evoked in the animal poems, the resulting impression is one of nearly overwhelming pessimism. De Lisle's animals are much more richly complex than those of Vigny and of Baudelaire, for example. Besides embodying a philosophical stance, de Lisle's animals conjure up an archaic and primeval world of force and instinct. Vigny's wolf and Baudelaire's albatross, on the other hand, the obvious products of the poets' civilized imaginations, convey their respective messages with unusual single-mindedness if not downright bluntness. De Lisle's animal poems, by contrast, emerge as more satisfactorily poetic precisely because of their greater implicitness. Unlike Vigny and Baudelaire, Leconte de Lisle has escaped quite handsomely from exploiting his subject matter as a thinly-clad literary device.

The thirty-six lines which comprise "Sacra fames" summarize the theory of evolution such as the poet understood it. The poem is a highly visual evocation of the law of universal extermination. The title is derived from Virgil's celebrated expression in Book Three of the *Aeneid: auri sacra fames* (the damnable thirst for gold), but de Lisle's sense is that of a sacred hunger rather than a damnable one. "Sacra fames" depicts a world devoid of all direction and morality and in which only the law of necessity reigns supreme. The setting is the Pacific Ocean where sharks are known to be particularly rapacious. Behind the idea of universal slaughter and destruction is that of complete hopelessness. The last two strophes translate in compelling terms Leconte de Lisle's sense of futility:

Go monster! For you are no different than we expect you to be, perhaps more hideous, ferocious or desperate. But take consolation in the knowledge that if you eat a man tomorrow, on another day, men will devour you in their turn. This sacred hunger is a long legitimate murder issuing from the depths of the shadows to the resplendent skies. And, whether it be man or shark, strangler or victim, oh! Death, before your image, both are equally innocent.[9]

"L'Albatros" depicts the bird who remains stalwart and impassive against the destructive forces of the wind at sea. The first twelve lines of the poem evoke the Atlantic Ocean, the birds, and the sperm whales as parts of a nature that is cruelly tossed by an unrelenting wind. The plaintive cries of the birds and the monstrous sobs of the whales allude to the tragedy of a suffering world. Only the albatross, referred to in the poem as king of the open skies, opposes the elements in an heroic confrontation. There is much in the stance of the stoical albatross that reminds us of the South American condor in the *Poèmes barbares.* Leconte de Lisle's expert manipulation of the alternating masculine and feminine rhymes in the twelve-foot lines produce an auditory prolongation which fittingly corresponds to the notion of space and grandeur that is conveyed in "L'Albatros." We are left with a final impression of the bird residing in a majestic solitude as it alone confronts the threatening winds.

What is heard is a confused whirling of sharp cries and of feathers being buffeted in the wind which drags them on to the crests of the foaming waves. The howling wind mixes with the monstrous sobs of the sperm whales whose massive foreheads receive hammering blows. Only the king of the open skies and of the shoreless seas dares to fly against the strong gusts. In a perfectly-timed powerful and steady thrust, with his eye staring intently beyond the livid fog and with his wings of iron outstretched in rigid fashion, he ventures into the whirlwind of raucous expanses, and, quietly, in the midst of all the terror, he comes, he passes and he disappears majestically into space.[10]

"L'Albatros" invites an obvious comparison with Baudelaire's well-known program poem of the same title in the *Fleurs du Mal.* Baudelaire's albatross is a poet—"The poet is like the prince of clouds." Somewhat ironically, the explicitness of Baudelaire's poem is much less deliberate in its objective. To be sure, both poets associate their birds with aspects of humanity, but Baudelaire's poem reduces his albatross to the single dimension of man. De Lisle's albatross conveys both a primal animal instinct and human attributes. The absence of the kind of philosophical intrusion such as the one contained in Baudelaire's poem endows de Lisle's poem with greater lyrical implicitness. The Parnassian poet relies more heavily upon the lugubrious atmosphere which "L'Albatros" evokes in order to make his point.

"L'Incantation du loup" conjures up much of the dignity and vitality which Leconte de Lisle associates with the primeval

world of animals. The poem describes a male wolf who sits stoically in the snows of the Hartz Mountains as he contemplates the
remains of his she-wolf and his cubs, the innocent victims of the
hunters' rifles. The wolf partakes of the same emotions and fears
of man: the death of his loved ones invests him with a sense of
emptiness. His thoughts are cast in the form of an incantation
that evokes a primal state of being free of the contamination of
man's "civilizing" influences:

And he, the chief of the Hartz mountain area, betrayed by the dwarf,
the giant, the he-goat, the sea-hawk and the wizard, remains in a
crouched position by the fire of peat and heather where a sinister
water boils in the bronze cauldron. His tongue fumes as it hangs out
from his deep carnivorous mouth, but he does not lick the blackened
blood which drips from his side. He raises his sharp head erect and he
grumbles, for in his entrails, a hatred burns and growls. Man, the old
butcher of his ancestors, of his cubs and of the regal she-wolf who
used to pour such passionate milk for them from her udder, haunts
his unalterably raging dream. A cinder of wood casts a reddish glim-
mer in his energetic pupil as his hairs stand up as stiff as nails. His
howling evokes the soul of former wolves who sleep in the glittering
magic of the moon.[11]

"L'Incantation du loup" differs conceptually and technically
from its initial source of inspiration, Vigny's "La Mort du loup."
Vigny's poem narrates the wolf hunt, the killing of the she-wolf
and her cubs, and winds up with a passage in which the lone
surviving wolf attempts a direct preachment on the superiority of
stoicism over other life attitudes. Man, in effect, becomes the
central focal point of "La Mort du loup" insomuch as the wolf
aims his morality directly at him. Moreover, Vigny's wolf is entirely anthropomorphic; he possesses no purely animalistic traits
whatsoever. It is interesting to note that both poems touch upon
the idea of isolation as a requisite for achieving a measure of
dignity. Yet, Leconte de Lisle's wolf poem emerges with considerably greater impact precisely because "L'Incantation du
loup" has avoided the casting of the animal on the plane of a
mere literary device.

IV *The Nature Evocations*

The sustained thematic rhythm to be found in the overwhelming number of poems which constitute the *Poèmes tragiques*

risked enveloping the collection in a uniform monotony. To avoid conferment of coldness and harshness upon the *Poèmes tragiques,* Leconte de Lisle sought to diversify his technical use of the lyric in a series of Malayan pantoums and villanellas. Both types of poems contribute importantly to the realization of formal variety and thematic cohesion of the collection. Appearing under the simple caption, "Pantouns malais," the five short poems which comprise this series represent considerable technical mastery over a poetic form which such poets as Victor Hugo and Baudelaire had not been able to achieve.[12] The pantoum is a chain verse form possessing an unlimited number of quatrain stanzas which are linked by having the second and fourth lines repeated as the first and the third lines of the following quatrain stanza. Leconte de Lisle makes adroit application of these intricate forms through a clever contrast of movement and stillness in these evocations of nature.

The first "Pantoun malais" describes in alternating couplets the action of an approaching storm and the amorous reveries of two lovers who remain indifferent to the threatening skies. The "Pantoun malais" begins and ends with the same line. The reveries of the lovers answer the dynamic movement of the storm in repeated refrains. Thus, the two themes, encountered elsewhere in the verse of de Lisle, are pursued almost simultaneously.

The lightning vibrates its tortuous arrow in the moving horizon of wavy clouds while you dream with your eyes half-closed on the mat of fine bark. In the moving horizon of wavy clouds, flashes of lightning illumine the foam of the wavy clouds, and you dream with your eyes half-closed in a hut which is perfumed by your body. Flashes of lightning illumine the foam of the wavy clouds and the shadows become a prey of the howling wind, while you dream and smile, my flower, in the hut which is perfumed by your body. The shadows become a prey of the howling wind and they are engulfed in the depth of some ravine, while you dream and smile, my flower, for your heart is bursting with some divine song.[13]

The opposing forces of clamorous movement and calm repose assert themselves in memorable fashion in this elegantly conceived and executed "Pantoun malais."

Exploited with equally felicitous results is the villanella, the Renaissance verse form used in the pastoral poetry of Jean Passerat. Comprised of a series of three-line stanzas and a concluding quatrain, the villanella pivots around two alternating rhymes. The rigid restrictions imposed by the metrical intricacy constituted a formidable challenge to the poet desiring to invest his lyrics with at least an apparent spontaneity. Leconte de Lisle uses the formal elegance of the villanella to frame a serious theme. The poem entitled, "Une Nuit noire, par un calme, sous l'Equateur," unveils the poet's pessimism in that it expresses a virtually ecstatic feeling for absorption into the void. What renders the villanella particularly memorable is that the theme is welded so ingeniously, rhythmically, to the formal and almost classical organization of the poem. The emotion that is expressed is delicately contained within the external sophisticated elegance of the villanella:

Time, space and number have all fallen from the black firmament into the dark motionless sea. A shroud of silence and of shadows, the night completely obliterates all time, space and number. Like a heavy and silent debris, the mind plunges into the sleeping void of the dark motionless sea. And in itself, with it, remembrance, dream, feeling, time, space and number become completely obliterated in the dark motionless sea.[14]

The gentle evocation of the memory of his young dead cousin, Elixenne de Lanux, in "Le Frais Matin dorait" provides the *Poèmes tragiques* with a welcome deviation from the generally harsh and embittered tone of the collection. De Lisle's recollection basks in a bittersweet lyrical expression which very nearly approaches that of a love poem. The nature that is nostalgically recalled blends neatly into the idealized portrait of the young lady whom he identifies as the physical embodiment of harmony, grace, charm, and sunlight. The accompanying themes of death and absence are conveyed with surprisingly subdued poignancy in *"Le Frais Matin dorait"*:

But Death, the virgin with the pale hands, embraced you before I did, my dearest! And ever since, I have lived far away from the clove trees and from the charming paths upon which your familiar footsteps can be heard, and far from my native skies in which the light of your beauty blossoms. It is as if centuries of alternating shadows and sunlight have passed, and I always gaze at the stars that are familiar to

me. In them, I see your beautiful eyes which used to gild the fresh
morning dew under the clove trees with the first rays of light.[15]

The softening effect of such poems as "Le Frais Matin dorait"
is soon canceled out, however, by the presence of such varied
expressions of Leconte de Lisle's pessimism as "A Un Poète mort,"
"La Maya" and "L'Illusion suprême." The sonnet commemorating
the memory of Théophile Gautier, "A Un Poète mort," cannot
refrain from the final intrusion in the closing tercet; de Lisle
addresses his dead friend in the following terms: "I envy you, in
your dark and peaceful grave, for being rid of life and for being
conscious no longer of the shame involved in thinking and of the
horror of being a man!" [16] Since all life becomes ultimately ne-
gated by death, all human aspiration toward permanence, in the
long run, becomes an excruciating illusion. The conclusion, asserted in "L'Illusion suprême," states in bitterness the tragedy of
man's death. For all of its formal containment, "L'Illusion suprême" betrays a lyric ingredient that is unmistakably linked to
the poet's attitude of bitter resentment. The last two stanzas of
this long poem underscore Leconte de Lisle's thinly-disguised
Romantic revolt against fate:

Ah! Youth, love, joy, the musical sounds of the sea and the forests, and
the breezes from the heavens, all of them carrying in their train an
insane Hope. What good are all of those things if they are not eternal?
So be it! The dust of man, a prey to time quickly passing by, his
pleasures, anguishes, struggles and remorse, the gods that he dreamed
up, and the stupid universe: all of those things are not worth as much
as the implacable peace of the dead.[17]

In the strict sense of the term, "La Maya" closes the *Poèmes
tragiques* since *Les Erinnyes,* published and performed on the
stage in 1873, was added only subsequently to the collection. Despite its brevity, "La Maya" constitutes an impressive summation
of the mood and temper which dictated the large majority of the
poems in the volume. Here, Leconte de Lisle delves once again
into his association of the brevity of existence with the illusion of
life. The poet's final statement in the *Poèmes tragiques* is as
devastating as it is categorical: life is but a foolish dream and an
illusion.

But what is the heart of ephemeral man, Oh! Maya, unless it is an immortal mirage of you? The centuries which have passed and the minutes which are about to happen, all become engulfed in your shadow in the same instant with our cries, our tears, and the blood of our veins. A flash, a sinister dream, a lying eternity. Ancient Life is inextinguishably constructed of an endless whirlwind of vain appearances.[18]

Left implicit in "La Maya" as well as in the other verse constituting the *Poèmes tragiques* is that art, man's formalization of his predicament, constitutes our only solace.

V *The* Erinnyes

Bearing the designation of poem 39, the *Erinnyes*, a verse adaptation of Aeschylus' *Oresteia*, first published in 1873, found its way into the 1881 edition of the *Poèmes tragiques*. The first public performance of Leconte de Lisle's dramatic poem took place on January 6, 1873 at the famous Odéon Theater in Paris. To alleviate some of the harshness residing in the poet's alexandrine verse, the theater director against the wishes of de Lisle, engaged the services of Jules Massenet for the composition of soft incidental music to be inserted at strategic intervals in the drama. The entire venture proved to be moderately successful and, by and large, the critical reaction of the time was embodied in the capsule comment which appeared in the January 8, 1873, issue of *Le Gaulois*: ". . . the first dramatic work of a genuine poet!" More recently, the Hellenist scholar, Fernand Desonay, has aptly described the *Erinnyes* as a drama of fierce beauty.[19]

Thematically, the *Erinnyes* blends neatly with the pessimistic conception of the *Poèmes tragiques*. From the very first scenes of the *Erinnyes* it becomes conspicuously plain that Leconte de Lisle's aim is not to translate Aeschylus, but to evoke a more primitive Greece than the one represented in the classical tragedy. The *Erinnyes* reveals a painstaking Parnassian concern for the reconstruction of authentic décor which is conveyed in the plastic quality of the language and the imagery. But de Lisle's account of Orestes' murder of Klytaimnestra underscores a brutality and a harshness which exemplified the Greek race before it had achieved Hellenic culture. The gods have been cursed in the *Erinnyes* for having invested man with anguish. What the

verse drama actually portrays is the terror of primitive man reduced to the state of bestiality. Such a design, of course, comple-
ments the Darwinian approach in such prominent evidence in the
Poèmes tragiques while not detracting from the collection's essential thematic unity.

The *Erinnyes* contains an interpretation of human destiny
whose most obvious pessimism is based on the Darwinian thesis
on heredity and environment. Leconte de Lisle conceives of his
tragic characters as half-men and half-beasts. In one scene, Cas-
sandra likens Agamemnon and his wife, Klytaimnestra, to a bull
next to a cow. The individuals which appear in de Lisle's dramatic
poem strike us as human beings who have hardly evolved on the
human level. The warriors are depicted as harsh "heroes" who
delight in sacking villages, in plundering, in strangling the vanquished, and in squashing children against the pavement. What
is understood by justice is in fact outright vengeance; Klytaimnestra's opening tirade in the third scene translates a sense of
barbaric fury which de Lisle sought to exploit in his dramatic
account:

Let the fire with a thousand tongues bristle the massive temples and
the blazing palaces. I hear the devastated Pallas swirling and the
crowd moaning as they fall from the heaps. The mothers howl with
horror at the sight of their babies' cradles being flung from the burning
roofs and smashing against the stones. The babies' bodies will soak
the soldiers' sandals with fresh blood. Oh! victory is sweet, and so is
revenge! Old men, give thanks to the gods for all of this, for how
many times did they catch me in the net of a vain dream or aspiration! We have to take advantage of our brief prosperity. After slightly
more than ten years of waiting and wishing, I see that the prize is
within my grasp. I must seize the occasion. Yes, the Master, my hus-
band, the king is returning to the blackened palace of the Tantalide
heroes, and since it will no doubt suit his convenience, we shall confront each other.[20]

Leconte de Lisle's conception of destiny differs significantly
from that of Aeschylus who regarded fate as a perplexing divinity
which remained alien to man. For the author of the *Erinnyes,*
destiny is construed as a force residing in man which compels
him to commit murder. De Lisle's dramatic poem is an adaptation in the fullest sense of that term. The *Erinnyes* interprets the
savage primitivism of the Greek character in distinctly nineteenth-

century terms and attitudes. The poem makes plain that Agamemnon has killed because his father before him had killed.
Likewise, his son, Orestes, will kill in his turn. The weight of
heredity and environment is readily discernible in de Lisle's
adaptation. Orestes' speech in the third scene of the second part
of the *Erinnyes* constitutes a good summary of what Leconte de
Lisle conceived as the primitive Greek hero. Orestes' ardor and
brutality are worthy of his mother's:

Since the time for action has come, it is a question of being quick
about it. I am consumed with a thirst for blood, and Destiny compels
me to do murder. Women, let one of you go in haste to the queen and
give her this message: "A traveller, who is unknown to us, daughter
of Leda, has arrived in Argos. He brings with him this news—and may
Zeus affirm that he speaks falsely—that Orestes rests languishing on
his funeral bed." Klytaimnestra will come running her heart over-
whelmed with joy.[21]

Like the overwhelming number of poems comprising the *Poèmes
tragiques*, the *Erinnyes* is an essentially lyrical rendition of Classical source materials. Indeed, the seemingly erudite reconstruction
of the dramatic setting is, in the long run, clearly subordinated to
the tone and the mood which Leconte de Lisle wishes to exploit.
As a powerful affirmation of the brutality which characterizes
man's struggle for life, the *Erinnyes* constitutes a fitting conclusion
to a collection of verse which underscores the tragically hopeless
dimension contained in such brutality.

CHAPTER 6

The Derniers Poèmes

THE *Derniers Poèmes* was published posthumously in 1895 under the scrupulous care and sympathetic editorship of the poet, José-Maria de Heredia. In an interview with Jules Huret concerning the state of lyricism in France, Heredia paid the following tribute to his friend: "Thanks to my cordial relationship with Leconte de Lisle, I have been able to benefit from the excellence of his precepts and his advice. I have also benefited much from his poetic practice. My greatest glory is that I have had the singular honor of being his pupil." [1] As editor for Leconte de Lisle's last poems, Heredia's most difficult task consisted in identifying the pieces that the poet had intended for eventual publication, and in determining which works he had disowned or dismissed as those associated with an ardent and youthful apprenticeship. The twenty-two poems which comprise the *Derniers Poèmes* explore no significant new ground, either technically or thematically. In a general way, these last poems take up with renewed enthusiasm many of the themes which dominated the *Poèmes antiques,* the *Poèmes barbares,* and the *Poèmes tragiques.* The *Derniers Poèmes* does underscore, however, a discernible attenuation or softening of the kind of harsh expression encountered so frequently in the *Poèmes tragiques.* Leconte de Lisle's last poems are complemented by a verse adaptation of Euripides' *Ion,* which was first published in 1889 under the title of *L'Apollonide.* As the poet's concluding statement, *L'Apollonide* contains de Lisle's fullest expression of the art of beauty.

A subsequent edition of the *Derniers Poèmes,* published by the Librairie Alphonse Lemerre in 1929, including Leconte de Lisle's prefaces and the studies on Béranger, Barbier, Lamartine, Vigny, Hugo, and Baudelaire which had appeared previously as separate essays in the *Nain jaune* under the rubric of "Poètes contem-

porains." Since we have already discussed these critical pronouncements at considerable length in Chapter 2, our examination here will concentrate on those poems which best exemplify
the themes and attitudes that dominate the collection. Our study
will end with an appraisal of the verse adaptation of Euripides'
Ion, L'Apollonide.

I   *Poetic Restatements*

If Leconte de Lisle experienced anguish which was born from
the acknowledgment of the absence of permanence in all human
phenomena, his severe invective against Christianity purported
to expose the Church's shameful exploitation of beliefs and
myths concerning the idea of eternity. His quarrel was with the
aggressive institutionality of organized religions rather than with
belief *per se.* Indeed, all of his poetry betrays, in the long run, a
cautious sympathy or admiration for the founders of new religions since the elaboration of religious idealism throughout the
ages revealed an explicit dissatisfaction with the solutons advanced by the pragmatic interpretations of various societies. But
such manifest sympathy remained substantially tempered by his
conclusion that religions emerge as the creations of different men
in response to specific psychological requirements made evident
during the various stages of man's evolution in society. Moreover,
each religion underscores some aspect of truth in its own time
since each translates a measure of man's aspiration toward an
absolute which can never be wholly overlooked.

The dramatic confusion which takes place between Christ and
the pope in "Les Raisons du Saint-Père" serves to clarify Leconte
de Lisle's anti-Christian sentiments. The Church that is evoked
in the poem is a vast political organization whose established
aim—the governance and subjugation of the believing masses—
has little or nothing to do with the promulgated aspirations of
its founder. Jesus enters as a specter into the pope's magnificent
chamber, listens quietly to his so-called vicar's tirade concerning
the nature and the function of the Church, then slowly but sadly
vanishes. Jesus, of course, represents the human aspiration toward permanence, and the pope exemplifies the practical concerns of Modernism. Much of the effectiveness of the poem as a
criticism of organized religion rests precisely in the quiet, almost
understated manner in which Leconte de Lisle unfolds the con-

frontation that takes place. The slow, deliberate pacing in the pope's exposition simulates the manipulation and organization required of the pragmatic leader. Implied in "Les Raisons du Saint-Père" is the idea that Christianity as a genuine religion is dead. Jesus, then, is the idealist dreamer, who has failed in his noble mission. There is little else for him to do but return in defeat to the heavens which he occupies, symbolically, with the gods of the other extinguished religions. The pope is triumphant in his cynical reign over souls which he controls with an absolute and terrifying power. The last five stanzas of "Les Raisons du Saint-Père" unveil with masterful control the poet's most eloquent argument against the exploitation of the people by organized Christianity. The pope addresses Jesus:

Christ, that is how we have refashioned your dream. We know more about man's lowly state than you did, and so we have taken your velvet, the keys and the sword, and we give you in return a frightened and subjugated people. But we have only recently realized this glorious ambition, and we must now suppress the perverted heretics. Refrain, in the future, from coming here and disturbing our nearly perfect accomplishments, for you risk loosening the net of subjugation which we have managed to spread over the universe. Rather, let our faith assert itself through the blood of our enemies and in the noises of our holy canticles. Do not interrupt our work again. Go back and reign in peace from the heights of your mystical heaven until at least the time of the completed centuries. For, we know very well that if we must disappear, one day, in the inundation of a revolutionary people, you will have us to thank for the fact that you will remain forever, Master, a god, the last god, in fact, of man's fabrication. The Holy Father stopped speaking, took his pectoral cross and with composure, he kissed it three times. Then, he traced the sign of the cross with his thumbs. And the specter of the image of Christ vanished slowly from the chamber.[2]

"La Paix des dieux" got its title from Louis Ménard's *Du Polythéisme hellénique* of 1863 which Leconte de Lisle had most certainly read. The poet of "La Paix des dieux," however, has twisted his friend Ménard's more optimistic context, and, from the optic of his later years, de Lisle declaims his final disillusionment in the quest for an eternal principle. To an important degree, the poem represents the aging poet's philosophic legacy to posterity. "La Paix des dieux" contains one of the finest illustra-

tions of the manner in which Leconte de Lisle managed to am-
plify his visionary and historical imagination in works which lay
claim to some degree of objectivity. The poem reviews an
impressive list of gods which, historically, have preoccupied man
from ancient Egyptian times to Modernism. The final conclusion
—that all deities remain the desperate creations of men goaded
by an intense desire for permanence—is framed, ingeniously, in
a perspective which alludes to no specific time or place. The
poet's comprehensive survey of the history of religions betrays a
personal desire to establish a faith in a divine principle which
could cancel out his own religious relativism. But in his ardent
aspiration to associate himself with a divinity which would con-
quer all time and space, man must unavoidably refer to his own
sense of observation of facts and acknowledge that the deity is
but an illusion fabricated by the heart, source of all life and
illusion:

Look! My heart is like the silent space where, in my loneliness, I ask
and answer my own question. This world, which is without purpose or
design, is where I exist. It envelops and wraps me in a heavy shroud.
Then, the vigilant companion of his dreams said to him: "Remain
senseless! For you would only plunge in vain into a celestial ocean that
has neither shore nor bottom. The divine charnel-house is in your own
heart. There too, are all of the dead gods and the dreams of the
men who conceived them, created them, adored them, and damned
them. For you voice which names them with their respective para-
dises and hells evokes them one by one." [3]

The poet's inquiry leads him directly to an acknowledgment
that all is illusion. But the personal anguish suffered by man will
ultimately end when the earth will disappear and enter into the
same unalterable peace in which the dead gods sleep. There is a
sought-for shrillness achieved through the rhythmic pacing of
"La Paix des dieux" which, at times, simulates the raucousness
associated with a voice in desperation reciting the history of
man's futile search for an absolute. The concluding strophes evoke
a sense of chilling finality in their equation of calm repose with
death. The poet addresses the spirit of the deceased gods and
receives their awesome reply in the resounding beat of his own
heart:

*   *   *

"You, in whom I had placed all of my fertile hope, and against whom I struggled in my proud freedom, if you are all dead, then, what else is there left for me to do in this world? I am the first believer and the old revolutionary." Man thought that he had heard a voice speak to his entire being. The voice spoke with a sad sobbing sound: "Nothing like this will ever be revived or born again, for the times will sweep all of that away wave upon wave. Nothing can ever again restore your faith: not your blasphemy, not your hatred, not your love. And know that henceforth, since you have now taken cognizance of the situation, that all of these finite specters were fabricated by you. But, go forth! Do not despair of your senseless work. This old mirage will soon disappear from sight, and everything will disappear—the world and all thought—in the unalterable peace into which the gods have returned." [4]

The generous reference made to the names of gods who have commanded the attention of man throughout history and the retention of antiquated spellings endow this very personal poem with at least an outer erudition which rescues it, ultimately, from emotional excess.

Poems such as "Les Yeux d'or de la nuit," "L'Aigu Bruissement," "Dans l'air léger," and "Toi par qui j'ai senti" are all at least partly rooted in a becalmed nostalgia for a past and a primitive nature which are identified with the peaceful void alluded to with increasing frequency in the poetry collections of Leconte de Lisle. "Les Yeux d'or de la nuit" evokes the sense of inexpressible peace which the poet recalls having experienced as a youth as he contemplated the stars from the perspective of the tropical island of Réunion. "L'Aigu Bruissement" is another such evocation, but this time the poet injects a note of pessimism as he underlines the association between youth and the birth of desire, man's fatal flaw. The concluding strophes summarize this impression from the perspective of his last declining years:

Everything, then, was sunlight, love, joy and harmony, and even though I was dazzled by this charming world, there was something within me like a groan, a painful sigh, a ceaseless lament that remained very distant and very vague but which made me bitterly sad. Within the bosom of your grace and beauty, Nature, I had never suffered nor guessed anything about man's predicament. Yet, I could feel the predestined man growing inside of me, and, seized with a sense of future anguish, I cried. I became terrified of life, and alas! I was terrified by the very fact that I had been born.[5]

Despite the lightness suggested by its formal elegance, the villanella entitled "Dans l'air léger" conveys a sadness and stillness which pervade the entire poem. The nostalgic verse which made its way into the *Derniers Poèmes* bespeaks a discernible calmness whose absence was conspicuously noticeable in the *Poèmes tragiques*. The sadness which emanates from "Dans l'air léger" is enshrined in an atmosphere of serenity. Despite allusions to a tropical setting, the final impression is one of a timeless landscape. Leconte de Lisle couches his personal feelings in the formal versification of the villanella. The quiet references made to the frail golden thread and to the evaporating perfume of the rose lead subtly to the conclusion on death in the final tercet.

In the cool air, in the pink-blue of the skies, a very frail golden thread makes its way up to the glittering bluffs which are sprayed by the dawn. A winged flower blooms in the morning when the bird awakens and flies away in the cool air, in the pink-blue of the skies. The bee is drinking up your soul, rose! The tamarind-tree is making noises on the bluffs which are sprayed by the dawn. The quivering mist does not dare to open out with fresh sighs in the cool air, in the pink-blue of the skies. And, the sea in which the skies find repose lets its vast and gentle sounds ascend to the bluffs which are sprayed by the dawn. But those divine eyes which I once loved have been closed for all time in the cool air, in the pink-blue of the skies.[6]

There is much in the villanella, a sixteenth-century form, that recalls Ronsard's celebrated odes to Cassandre and well-known sonnets to Hélène. The kind of remoteness which Leconte de Lisle attempted to achieve in all of his poetry collections is realized most eloquently in "Dans l'air léger."

The two quatrains that comprise the last poem of the collection, "Toi par qui j'ai senti," sum up Leconte de Lisle's philosophy that identifies love and beauty as man's only solace in existence. The mood and tone which pervade "Toi par qui j'ai senti" are representative of the kind of tempered emotions which inform the *Derniers Poèmes*.

You, through whom I have been able to feel alive but for too brief a time, and who have revived my youth and made my heart bloom again, may you be forever blessed! For I love, and now, I am able to die because I have realized the best and the most beautiful of my aspirations. Your beautiful eyes, which I adore, still envelop me today in their gentle charm. They have given me back the mornings of my days. You may now not remember me, but I shall see you always until the day I die.[7]

II *L'Apollonide*

Composed in 1889, and first performed on the stage with incidental music by Massenet in 1986, *L'Apollonide* was judiciously selected to complement the *Derniers Poèmes*. A verse drama based on Euripides' *Ion*, *L'Apollonide* contains Leconte de Lisle's complete thoughts on the idea and the cult of beauty. It is interesting to note that in *L'Apollonide*, the world of a harsh fatality is skirted by the poet without his ever actually succumbing to it. Euripides himself was the most irreverent of the Classical dramatists: his tragedies lash out satirical thrusts at the divinities of Mount Olympus.[8] What Leconte de Lisle sets out to achieve in his dramatic poem is the artistic celebration of the Ancient Greek conception of art and beauty. Ion, son of Apollo, represents the idealization of the virtues of the future Ionian race. *L'Apollonide* minimizes the religious undertones in the poem by placing more emphasis on the aesthetic cult surrounding the lives of Apollo and his son, Ion.

By and large, Leconte de Lisle follows closely Euripides' dramatization of the story of the son of Apollo and of Kréousa, the queen of Attica. The latter, after having been seduced by the god, Apollo, gave birth to a son, Ion, whom she subsequently abandoned. Found one day in a basket, Ion was brought to the temple of Apollo where he was raised. Meanwhile, Kréousa married Xouthos, king of Attica, who had heroically come to the aid of Athens in a previous war. Without child from this union, Kréousa presents herself at the temple of Apollo to consult with the Oracles. She briefly encounters Ion who is a guardian at the temple, and the two experience a natural and instinctive sympathy for each other. In a touching scene, Kréousa recounts to Ion how she had been compelled by the gods to abandon her infant son. Ion pities her and relates to her the story of his own abandonment. Xouthos, who had penetrated the temple, comes out greeting Ion as his "son." The Oracle, Pythia, advised Xouthos to consider as his progeny the first person he would meet leaving the temple. Ion feels in no way drawn to Xouthos, and he hesitates to proclaim the man who had previously abandoned him. Ion goes to Athens in disguise as the guest of Xouthos. Despairing over the fact that the stranger (unknown to her at this time) will install himself on the throne of Attica rather than her lost son, Kréousa plots to have the stranger poisoned. Foiled in her attempt, Kréousa is condemned to endure torture before dying at the hands of Ion. At this point, the god, Apollo, intervenes and reveals the real identity of Ion. A reconciliation takes place, and all ends well.

A warm and luminous atmosphere permeates de Lisle's *Apollonide* and it is clear from the opening scene that de Lisle is paying tribute to the personification of the Greek genius. His dramatic adaptation of Euripides' drama underscores all of the characteristics which he has long associated with Classical Athens and the cult of beauty. His hero is gentle, humane, and exhibits a perfect balance and moderation in his desires. He is even made to lash out, occasionally, against the arbitrariness of the gods on Mount Olympus. In Euripides' version of the story of Ion, the foundling stands guard in the temple of Apollo out of gratitude and a sense of duty. In *L'Apollonide,* the poet makes it plain that is it Ion's love of art and beauty which motivates his activity in the temple. The antistrophe in the second scene of the first part calls attention to the natural beauty which occupies the mind of the son of Apollo:

Oh! spring-wells, which will never be drained empty, you tipple and sing so harmoniously in moss among the lilies that are heavy with dew on the slope of the solitary, enchanted mountain! Fresh spring water! From the thresholds and from the Pythian steps, pour out the treasures of your azure-blue urns. May the flow of my fateful days be like yours: chaste and pure. But a sudden shadow and an indistinct murmuring can be seen and heard coming from the snowy peaks and emerging from the foliage. This shadow and these sounds rise in the cloudless heaven above the temple and the woods. I am witnessing the morning flight of the birds.[9]

Ion is presented as the epitome of artistic measure and emotional temperance. He wishes to remain in calm contentment, far from the vainglorious temptations of other men. The chorus of women in the following scene evokes the almost ethereal beauty of Apollo's temple. When Ion must take leave of this sanctuary to join Xouthos, he voices regret for that which he must leave behind: the softness of the earth, the splendor of the marble, and the gentleness of the birds which surround the place of worship. In Scene Four of the second part, a chorus of Oreads pays the following tribute to the departing archer, Ion:

Handsome archer, your light features will no longer follow the flight of the wild ring-doves in the resonant air above the forest's foliage which rustles and which is gilded by the dawn. And, never again will the smell of the sap which perfumes the thickets bewitch your gentle dreams! Since you are going to leave the holy temple and the spring-well which tipples to the Pythian rocks, we bid you farewell! May the dancing chorus of Oreads give pleasure to your eyes for one last time![10]

Despite his acute sensitivity to beauty, Leconte de Lisle's Ion may in no way be interpreted as an emasculation of Euripides' hero. The handsome archer of *L'Apollonide* exhibits admirable courage and determination in at least two instances; one, when he threatens Xouthos with a sword as the latter attempts to embrace him (against the religious prescriptions of the temple); the other, when he prepares to carry out, unflinchingly, the orders of the gods by acting as Kréousa's executioner. But de Lisle's chief concern in this dramatic poem is to unfold what he considers to be the innate superiority of an Antiquity which fostered and encouraged the cult of art and beauty. The aesthetic cult described in *L'Apollonide* serves as a mitigating force against the harshness and arbitrariness of fate. The mildness with which Ion speaks to the soldiers of Xouthos, who have offered him the sceptre, reveals a fundamentally aesthetic sense of values which corresponds strikingly to that of the leading Parnassian poets. His words betray a purity and an innocence which serve as implicit rejections of the more worldly and pragmatic considerations. In the closing scene of the first part of *L'Apollonide*, Ion makes the following reply to the entreaty of Xouthos that he attempt to earn the laurels of the warrior for his head:

The laurels which grow here are more beautiful and more resplendently verdant in the dawn than elsewhere. They are as soft as a lyre gently singing out in the echoing wind. But the divine Muse, with her beautiful hands, will never place such laurels on inhuman foreheads.[11]

Ion's speeches in the same scene provide a dramatic antithesis to those intonated and recited by Xouthos' warriors. The latter invoke the spirit of Gorgô, the immortal monster, to urge them on to battle. In immediate contrast, Ion's think nostalgically of myrrh and incense and the song of birds in brilliantly reassuring horizons. But, in the end, catastrophes are averted—Kréousa fails to kill her son, unknowingly, and Ion is not required to execute his mother, unknowingly—thanks to the intervention of Apollo or Loxias, the sun god. Under the gaze of Apollo, art and beauty will flourish. The work ends appropriately with an invocation by the Muses who remind man that he should quest the pleasures of beauty, the physical embodiment of permanence, in peace and serenity.

We are the sacred Virgins, the delight of the vast universe, with mitres of gold and green laurel crowns and with inspiration always on our lips. Man, worried and ephemeral, and the Ouranid, far up in the skies, are illumined by our flames. Sometimes, our immortal songs even gladden the hearts of men who inhabit the darkened Hades.[12]

The closing invocations to Athens and the hymn to Apollo, the creating force of life, constitute an harmonious crowning point to Leconte de Lisle's idea of the cult of beauty as it is realized in art. But, despite the attenuation in mood so much in evidence in *L'Apollonide,* the dramatic poem falls considerably short of being a masterpiece in the true sense of the term. The interspersing of numerous speeches and tirades arguing in favor of art and beauty reveals the heavy hand of the poet and finally detracts from the drama's sustained progression. All of the speeches display a single-mindedness that renders them ultimately monotonous. There can be no denying that Leconte de Lisle's admiration for Ancient Greece stems from an unabashed infatuation with a notion that is as much rooted in his own imagination as in historical fact. The topological references to Greece in *L'Apollonide* belie those of reality; de Lisle speaks constantly of a lush nature setting, of rippling streams and heavy-dewed mosses. Just as his entire poetic outlook as a Parnassian poet seeks to temper intuition, emotion, and imagination by generous reference to reality and historical fact, the *Apollonide* weaves out of personal attitudes and a cognizance of Ancient Greece a poetic and idealized portrait of a world which remains equidistant between man's unlimited aspiration and his modest achievement. *L'Apollonide* typifies Leconte de Lisle's major attitudes as a poet who chose spiritual exile from the Industrial Age in which he lived.

CHAPTER 7

Conclusion

LECONTE de Lisle's aristocratic dismissal of all contemporary values as both dated and demeaning constituted an explicit endorsement of the attitude of Art for Art's Sake which Théophile Gautier had assumed during the early 1830's. De Lisle's contempt for the spirit of Modernism stemmed from an excruciating awareness of the ultimate irreconciliability which existed between man's unbounded aspiration and his limited achievement. His personal experiences served to corroborate a metaphysical pessimism which had already begun to assert itself in him during the mid-1840's. The failure of the Second Republic in 1851 and the pervasive influence of industry upon all facets of nineteenth-century society underscored for him the degeneracy into which modern civilization had fallen. Increasingly, the leading French Romantic poets, in their feverish attempts to fashion a new social equilibrium, contaminated their respective cosmogonic explications of man's predicament with a utilitarianism that tainted and diluted their lyrical expression. In de Lisle's view, the modern poet had allowed his primitive intuitive sense to become blunted by purely pragmatic considerations. To put it plainly, such preoccupations impeded the leading Romanticists from articulating satisfactorily man's primitive longing for an ideal state of being. To restore to lyricism its lost spontaneity and its primal force, the poet would have to strive to rid himself of all moral and didactic intentions.

As far as Leconte de Lisle was concerned, the poet played an historical and scientific role in his attempt to rediscover for modern man the original sources from which all beauty and meaning proceed. Clearly, the superior artist was the one who exercised constant vigilance in preserving the truly educational function of lyricism free from any kind of social, political, or religious encroachment. He defined the poet and his mission in the preface to the *Poètes contemporains*: "He perceives things in a glimpse further, higher and more profoundly than anyone else because he contemplates the ideal through visible beauty which he proceeds to concentrate and to enshrine in expression which is appropriate, precise and memorable." All of Leconte de Lisle's poetic theory and practice emanate from the manifesto-pronouncement of the preface. As eventual leader of what may be termed the Parnassian movement during the 1860's and 1870's, he articulated a conception of poetry which was founded on historical and scientific knowledge rather than on any loosely invoked inspiration. The scientific spirit of the age of Positivism as well as the discoveries of Lamarck and Darwin dislodged whatever absolute idealism he may have nurtured privately. Leconte de Lisle advocated a *rapprochement* between poetry and scientific method. Such an alliance, he felt, would ensure lyric expression with a sufficiently objective quality which would rescue it from deteriorating into blatant subjectivity. As principal contributor to Alphonse Lemerre's three editions of the *Parnasse contemporain,* Leconte de Lisle sought to renew the rhetoric of lyrical expression with tighter formal techniques which would tend to balance inspiration and ideas with verbal expression. With José-Maria de Heredia, he held that form constiuted more than a means of translating the aesthetic ideal: it was actually the means by which it could be achieved.

If the present actually deterred the poet from his true inspiration and function, the past provided him with examples of heroism and beauty worthy of human emulation. The task of the lyricist was essentially that of the epic poet: to record the finality of life and death in aesthetically pleasing language. Leconte de Lisle's unwillingness to separate form from thematic content led him ultimately to outlaw unrestricted imagery and metaphor. As a result, his verse proceeds by statement and description rather than by the suggestive allusiveness of symbols. Unlike Baudelaire and the later Symbolists, there is little or no room for ambiguity in de Lisle's poetry. While it is true that his name has been frequently associated with such terms as objectivity, impassibility and antimodernism, it should be underlined that de Lisle aimed to achieve but a measure of such attitudes in order to exteriorize his personal feelings and reactions. His four collections of verse, the *Poèmes antiques,* the *Poèmes barbares,* the *Poèmes tragiques,* and the *Derniers Poèmes* all betray in varying degrees of intensity a metaphysical pessimism that is welded to his personal vision of existence. His best poetry bespeaks a nostalgia for a world in which the painful awareness of human limitation is eradicated. His poems can, by no stretch of the imagination, be construed as scientific or objective recreations of ancient or barbaric civilizations. More frequently than not, de Lisle's excursions into the past afford him the possibility of tempering his own emotional impulse with sobering surface allusions to the periphery of reality.

Technically, Leconte de Lisle's poetry rose in open reaction to the extreme subjectivity of French Romanticism. As head of the Parnassian movement, he instituted formal reforms which were meant to endow lyric expression with a greater measure of objectivity. Many of de Lisle's innovative uses of meter, rhythm, and rhyme were destined to survive in French Symbolism which flourished in the 1880's and 1890's. Leconte de Lisle's Parnassianism may be described as a noteworthy transitional link between Romanticism and Symbolism.

Notes and References

Chapter One

1. Mlle de Riscourt de Lanux was a descendant of a certain marquis de Lanux who had settled in Réunion (then Bourbon) in 1720. Leconte de Lisle's mother was also related to the poet, Evariste-Désiré de Parny (1753–1814) who also resided on the island. He was the author of several collections of poems.

2. See Maurice Souriau, *Histoire du Parnasse* (Paris: Spes, 1929), p. 147: "This predilection for the *Fables* is sufficient explanation in itself for the particular beauty residing in Leconte de Lisle's verse which appears to be a kind of Romanticism immersed in Classical sources."

3. *Discours de réception à l'Académie Française,* delivered on March 31, 1887.

4. Leconte de Lisle's examiners termed his written and oral performances in Greek language and literature as mediocre. See Fernand Desonay, *Le Rêve hellénique chez les poètes parnassiens* (Paris: Champion, 1928), p. 141.

5. Among the teachers at the University of Rennes who influenced de Lisle's thinking were Charles Labitte (primitive literature), Xavier de Marmier (for the series subsequently published as the *Chants populaires du nord*), Emile de la Bigne Villeneuve (biblical literature), and Théodore Henri Martin (Greek and Latin tragedy). See also: Alison Fairlie, *Leconte de Lisle's Poems on the Barbarian Races* (Cambridge, England: At the University Press, 1947), pp. 3–7.

6. Quoted by Pierre Flottes, *Leconte de Lisle: l'homme et l'oeuvre* (Paris: Hatier-Boivin, 1954), pp. 16–17.

7. It should be pointed out, however, that in the first issue of *La Variété* (April, 1840), Professor Alexandre Nicholas argued for a Christian rather than a Pagan (in the sense of Classical) direction for the journal.

8. "André Chénier: de la poésie lyrique à la fin du XVIIIe siècle," republished in *Leconte de Lisle: articles, préfaces, discours,* Edgard Pich, editor (Paris: Société d'Edition: Les Belles Lettres, 1971), p. 54.

9. *Contes en prose: impressions de jeunesse* (Société normande du livre illustré, 1910), p. 157.

10. In this respect, see Leconte de Lisle's article, "La Justice et le Droit," in the October 24, 1846, issue of *La Démocratie pacifique.*

11. Louis Ménard's *Prométhée délivré* was published in 1843.

12. Quoted in Maurice Leblond's *Leconte de Lisle d'après des documents nouveaux* (Paris: Mercure de France, 1906), pp. 229–30.

13. Irving Putter states the case of de Lisle's situation with pungency in *The Pessimism of Leconte de Lisle: Sources and Evolution* (Berkeley: University of California Press, 1954), p. 126: "The poet is thirty. His dream of social justice, never well-assured, always clouded by personal anxieties, has now disintegrated, leaving him face to face with his desolate vision of the universe."

14. Quoted in Pierre Flottes, *op. cit.*, pp. 87–89.

15. Irving Putter, *op. cit.*, p. 160.

16. *Les Origines de la France contemporaine* II (Paris: Hachette, 1907), 176.

17. Ernest Renan, "Averroès et l'averroïsme," in *Oeuvres complètes* III (Paris: Calmann-Lévy, 1947–1958), 15: "The characteristic feature of the nineteenth century is that it replaced the dogmatic method by the historical method in all of the studies pertaining to the human mind."

18. For an account of the development of the Parnassian movement, see Maurice Souriau's *Histoire du Parnasse.*

19. Irving Putter, *op. cit.*, p. 235.

20. See Leconte de Lisle's letter to José-Maria de Heredia dated September 24, 1874, and quoted in Miodrag Ibrovac's *José-Maria de Heredia: sa vie; son œuvre* (Paris: Presses universitaires, 1923), p. 138.

Chapter Two

1. "Les Femmes de Byron," *La Phalange* IV (September, 1846), 186: "Poets are the lovers and revealers of the infinite sense of beauty."

2. See Edgard Pich's edition of *Leconte de Lisle: articles, préfaces, discours,* pp. 8–12.

3. Published in its entirety in the December 1, 1876 edition of the *Revue des deux mondes.*

4. "I therefore do not believe that it is absolutely impossible for the epic to be reborn some day." Leconte de Lisle's attitude towards the possibility of such a renascence contrasts with the attitude of Thalès Bernard who believed that the poet would be immediately restored to "the state of grace" by a veritable return to nature. Cf. Edgard Pich, *op. cit.*, p. 118.

5. Charles Baudelaire, "L'Ecole païenne" in *L'Art romantique* (Paris: Garnier, 1962), p. 581.

6. This passage is quoted in French in Elliott M. Grant's *French Poetry and Modern Industry, 1830–1870* (Cambridge, Mass.: Harvard University Press, 1927), p. 86.

7. Ernest Renan, "La Poésie de l'exposition" in the November 27, 1855 issue of the *Journal des Débats.*

8. Armand de Pontmartin, *Causeries littéraires* (Paris: Lévy, 1854), p. 98.

9. Gustave Flaubert, *Correspondance* II (Paris: Charpentier, 1899), 199.

10. Edgard Pich, *op. cit.*, pp. 128–29.

11. See Thalès Bernard, *Histoire de la poésie* (Paris: Dentu, 1864), p. 60, in which he admonishes French writers who took pleasure in trapping their readers in the abyss of Indian mysticism which, in his estimation, destroys the concept of man.

12. *Le Nain jaune,* connected with the regime of Louis-Napoleon, was edited by Théophile Silvestre at the time when Leconte de Lisle published his five essays subsequently known as the *Poètes contemporains.* 1864 was also the year in which the poet received a pension from the emperor's personal budget. The question arose whether or not de Lisle was attempting to show some kind of allegiance to the Second Empire. The essay on Hugo, however, is a laudatory one, while the essay on the regime's public hero, Béranger, is rather devastating. Be that as it may, the articles which appeared in the *Nain jaune* confirmed the fact that the Parnassian movement evolved around the personality of Leconte de Lisle.

13. The *avant-propos* and the five essays on Béranger, Barbier, Lamartine, Hugo, and Vigny—as well as a separate essay on Baudelaire—have been collected and published in the postface to the posthumous collection, *Derniers Poèmes.*

14. See Edgard Pich, *op. cit.*, p. 16. He detects a Schopenhauerian influence at this juncture, claiming that de Lisle gives indication of having read the philosopher in the still unedited *Cahiers.*

15. Béranger had rescued de Lisle from financial embarrassment in 1853.

16. *William Shakespeare* is an exposition of Hugo's ideas on philosophy, politics, and literature in 1864.

17. For a fuller discussion of Leconte de Lisle and the French Academy, see Irving Putter's "Leconte de Lisle and the French Academy," *Modern Language Quarterly* (December, 1966), 418–30 and *La Dernière Illusion de Leconte de Lisle: lettres inédites à Emilie Leforestier* (Berkeley: University of California Press, 1968).

18. Edgard Pich, *op. cit.*, p. 217.

Chapter Three

1. Richard Chadbourne, "The Generation of 1848: Four Writers and their Affinities," *Essays in French Literature* V (1968), 8.

2. The remaining pieces in *Poèmes et poésies* were transferred to the *Poèmes barbares.*

3. "Khirôn" (from Part II):

  Et moi, contemporain de jours prodigieux,
  En plaignant les vaincus j'applaudissais les Dieux,
  Certain de leur justice, et pourtant dans mon âme
  Roulant un noir secret brûlant comme la flamme,
  Et je laissais flotter au bord des flots assis,
  Dans le doute et l'effroi mes esprits indécis;
  Songeur, je me disais:—Sur les cimes neigeuses
  L'aigle peut déployer ses ailes orageuses,
  Et, l'œil vers Hélois incessamment tendu,
  Briser l'effort des vents dans l'espace éperdu;
  Car sa force est cachée en sa lutte éternelle;
  Il se complaît, s'admire, et s'agrandit en elle.
  Avide de lumière, altéré de combats,
  Le sol est toujours noir, les cieux sont toujours bas;
  Il vole, il monte, il lutte, et sa serre hardie
  Saisit le triple éclair dont le feu l'incendie!

4. Irving Putter, *The Pessimism of Leconte de Lisle: The Work and the Time*, p. 179.

5. "Khirôn" (from Part V):

  Dans ma jeune saison que la Terre était belle!
  Les grandes eaux naguère avaient de leurs limons
  Reverdi dans l'Aither les pics altiers des monts.

6. The concluding stanzas from "La Vénus de Milo":

  Iles, séjour des Dieux! Hellas, mère sacrée!
  Oh! que ne suis-je né dans le saint Archipel,
  Aux siècles glorieux où la Terre inspirée

  Voyait le Ciel descendre à son premier appel!
  Si mon berceau, flottant sur la Thétis antique,
  Ne fut point caressé de son tiède cristal,
  Si je n'ai point prié sous le fronton attique,
  Beauté victorieuse, à ton autel natal;

  Allume dans mon sein la sublime étincelle,
  N'enferme point ma gloire au tombeau soucieux;
  Et fais que ma pensée en rythmes d'or ruisselle,
  Comme un divin métal au moule harmonieux.

7. See especially: Putter, *op. cit.*, p. 254, and Fernand Desonay, *op. cit.*, p. 294.

8. Alexandre Embiricos, *Leconte de Lisle* (Thonon-les-Bains: Société d'Edition savoyarde, 1941), p. 116.

9. The concluding dialogues of "Chant alterné":

  Les sages hésitaient; l'âme fermait son aile;

> *L'homme disait au ciel un triste et morne adieu:*
> *J'ai fait germer en lui l'Espérance éternelle,*
> *Et j'ai guidé la terre au devant de son Dieu!*
>
> *O coupe aux flots de miel où s'abreuvait la terre,*
> *Volupté! Monde heureux plein de chants immortels!*
> *Ta fille bien aimée, errante et solitaire,*
> *Voit l'herbe de l'oubli croître sur ses autels.*
>
> *Amour, amour sans tache, impérissable flamme!*
> *L'homme a fermé son coeur, le monde est orphelin.*
> *Ne renaîtras-tu pas dans la nuit de son âme,*
> *Aurore du seul jour qui n'ait pas de déclin?*

10. From the opening scene of "Hypatie et Cyrille":

> *Non! j'ai trop entendu leurs cris barbares! Non,*
> *Je ne m'abuse point. Tous maudissent ton nom.*
> *Leur âme est furieuse, et leur face enflammée.*
> *Ils te déchiront, ma fille bien-aimée,*
> *Ces monstres en haillons, pareils aux animaux*
> *Impurs, qui vont toujours prophétisant les maux,*
> *Qui, rongés de désirs et consumés d'envie,*
> *Blasphèment la beauté, la lumière et la vie!*

11. His *Histoire populaire du Christianisme,* published in 1871, is a scathing denunciation of modern-day Christianity which he feels exerts an evil social and moral influence.

12. From Scenes 3 and 4 of "Hypatie et Cyrille":

> *Je ne puis oublier, en un silence lâche,*
> *Le soin de mon honneur et ma suprême tâche,*
> *Celle de confesser librement sous les cieux*
> *Le beau, le vrai, le bien, qu'ont révélés les Dieux.*
> *Depuis deux jours déjà, comme une écume vile,*
> *Les Moines du désert abondent dans la ville,*
> *Pieds nus, la barbe inculte et les cheveux souillés,*
> *Tout maigris par le jeûne, et du soleil brûlés.*
> *On prétend qu'un projet sinistre et fanatique*
> *Amène parmi nous cette horde extatique.*
> *C'est bien. Je sais mourir, et suis fière du choix*
> *Dont m'honorent les Dieux une dernière fois.*
> *Cependant je rends grâce à ta sollicitude*
> *Et n'attends plus de toi qu'un peu de solitude.*
>
> . . . .
>
> *Je vais être immortelle. Adieu!*

13. Irving Putter, *The Pessimism of Leconte de Lisle: The Work and Time,* pp. 288–89.

14. *Ibid.,* p. 329.

15. *Ibid.*, p. 330. Especially: "Leconte de Lisle's desire for death shares with Nirvana the idea of liberation, but apart from this, there is no positive effort in the poems corresponding to Buddhist doctrine, no serene, willful attempt to nullify desire, and no acceptance of suffering, to say nothing of altruistic feeling for humanity."

16. The refrain from "Sûryâ":

> *Ta demeure est au bord des océans antiques,*
> *Maître! Les grandes Eaux lavent tes pieds mystiques.*

17. Leconte de Lisle corrected "La Mort de Valmiki" twice—once in 1886, and once in 1890. Our references are to the definitive edition. The closing lines from "La Mort de Valmiki":

> *L'esprit ne sait plus rien des sens ni de soi-même.*
>
> *Et les longues fourmis traînant leur ventre blême,*
> *Ondulent vers leur proie inerte, s'amassant,*
> *Circulant, s'affaissant, s'enflant et bruissant*
> *Comme l'ascension d'une écume marine.*
>
> *Elles couvrent ses pieds, ses cuisses, sa poitrine,*
> *Mordent, rongent la chair, pénètrent par les yeux*
> *Dans la concavité du crâne spacieux,*
> *S'engouffrent dans la bouche ouverte et violette,*
> *Et de ce cops vivant font un roide squelette*
> *Planté sur l'Himavat comme un Dieu sur l'autel,*
> *Et qui fut Valmiki, le poète immortel,*
> *Dont l'âme harmonieuse emplit l'ombre où nous sommes*
> *Et ne se taira plus sur les lèvres des hommes.*

18. See Joseph Vianey, *Les Sources de Leconte de Lisle* (Montpellier: Coulet, 1907), p. 63

19. The beginning of "Bhâgavat":

> *"Trois sages méditaient, assis sur des roseaux."*

20. The sages's lament in "Bhâgavat":

> *Cri de l'âme, sanglot du cœur supplicié,*
> *Qui t'entend sans frémir d'amour et de pitié*
> *Qui ne pleure sur toi, magnanime faiblesse,*
> *Esprit qu'un aiguillon divin excite et blesse,*
> *Qui t'ignore toi-même et ne peux te saisir,*
> *Et sans borner jamais l'impossible désir,*
> *Durant l'humaine nuit qui jamais ne s'achève,*
> *N'embrasses l'Infini qu'en un sublime rêve?*
> *O douloureux Esprit, dans l'espace emporté,*
> *Altéré de lumière, avide de beauté,*
> *Qui retombes toujours de la hauteur divine*
> *Où tout être vivant cherche son origine,*
> *Et qui gémis, saisi de tristesse et d'effroi,*
> *O conquérant vaincu, qui ne pleure sur toi.*

21. Angira's opening speech in "Bhâgavat":

J'ai vécu, l'oeil fixé sur la source de l'Etre,
Et j'ai laissé mourir mon coeur pour mieux connaître.

22. Putter, *op. cit.*, 321.

23. From the concluding part of "Bhâgavat":

Tu souris, Bhâgavat, à ces âmes sublimes.
Toi-même, ô Dieu puissant, dispensateur des biens,
Dénouas de l'Esprit les suprêmes liens;
Et dans son sein sans borne, océan de lumière,
Ils s'unirent tous trois à l'Essence première,
Le principe et la fin, erreur et vérité,
Abîme de néant et de réalité
Qu'enveloppe à jamais de sa flamme féconde
L'invisible Mâyâ, créatrice du monde,
L'espoir et souvenir, le rêve et la raison,
L'unique, l'éternelle et sainte illusion.

24. The last two stanzas from "La Vision de Brahma":

Brahma! tel est le rêve où ton esprit s'abîme.
N'interroge donc plus l'auguste Vérité:
Que serais-tu, sinon ma propre vanité
Et le doute secret de mon néant sublime?

Et sur les sommets d'or du divin Kaîlaça,
Où nage dans l'air pur le vol des blancs génies,
L'inexprimable Voix cessant ses harmonies,
La Vision terrible et sainte s'effaça.

25. See Souriau, *op. cit.*, p. 198. Also: Gladys Falshaw, *Leconte de Lisle et l'Inde* (Paris: D'Arthez, 1923), p. 168.

26. The last strophes of "Midi":

Non loin, quelques boeufs blancs, couchés parmi les herbes,
Bavent avec lenteur sur leurs fanons épais,
Et suivent de leurs yeux languissants et superbes
Le songe intérieur qu'ils n'achèvent jamais.

Homme si, le coeur plein de joie et d'amertume,
Tu passais vers midi dans les champs radieux
Fuis! la nature est vide et le soleil consume:
Rien n'est vivant ici, rien n'est triste ou joyeux.

Viens! Le soleil te parle en paroles sublimes;
Dans sa flamme implacable absorbe-toi sans fin;
Et retourne à pas lents vers les cités infimes,
Le coeur trempé sept fois dans le néant divin.

27. Charles-Augustin de Sainte-Beuve, *Causeries du lundi* V (Paris: Garnier [1944]), 314.

28. Putter, *op. cit.*, p. 270.
29. Stanzas 24–26 from "Dies Irae":

Où sont les Dieux promis, les formes idéales,
Les grands cultes de pourpre et de gloire vêtus,
Et dans les cieux ouvrant ses ailes triomphales
La blanche ascension des sereines Vertus?

Les Muses, à pas lents, Mendiantes divines,
S'en vont par les cités en proie au rire amer.
Ah! c'est assez saigner sous le bandeau l'épines,
Et pousser un sanglot sans fin comme la Mer!

Oui! le Mal éternel est dans sa plénitude!
L'air du siècle est mauvais aux esprits ulcérés.
Salut, Oubli du Monde et de la multitude!
Reprends-nous, ô Nature, entre tes bras sacrés!

30. Théophile Gautier, *Histoire du Romantisme* (Paris: Charpentier, 1884), pp. 333–34.

Chapter Four

1. Alison Fairlie, *Leconte de Lisle's Poems on the Barbarian Races*, p. 3: "The first poems on the barbarian races were then begun at about the time of the publication of the *Poèmes antiques*: they were not dictated by any deliberately planned contrast with the world of the Greeks, but rather, they mark, as we shall see, the extension of the poet's interest in new legends and new settings in which he could find many of the same qualities to admire and the same inevitable destruction to deplore."
2. See Joseph Vianey, *Les Poèmes Barbares de Leconte de Lisle* (Paris: Nizet, 1955), pp. 7–19.
3. Alison Fairlie, *op. cit.*, p. 170.
4. Joseph Vianey, *op. cit.*, pp. 165–73.
5. The speech of the hunters in "Le Runoîa":

Qu'ils meurent, s'il le faut! Dans les steppes natales
En chasserons-nous moins le cerf au bond leger?
Vienne le jour marqué par les Runas fatales!
La querelle des Dieux est pour nous sans danger.
Pourvu que l'ours rusé se prenne à nos embûches,
Que l'arc ne rompe past, et qu'un chaud hydromel
Au prompt soleil du Nord fermente dans les cruches,
Frères, la vie est bonne à vivre sous le ciel!
Vivons, ouvrons nos cœurs aux ivresses nouvelles;
Chasser et boire en paix, voilà l'unique bien.
Buvons! Notre sang brûle et nos femmes sont belles;
Demain n'est pas encore, et le passé n'est rien.

6. The closing lines of "Le Runoïa":

> Seul des siens, à travers cette ruine immense,
> L'éternel Runoïa descendit en silence.
> Dépossédé d'un monde, il lança sur la mer
> Sa nacelle d'airain, sa barque à fond de fer;
> Et tandis que le vent, d'une brusque rafale,
> Tordait les blancs flocons de sa barbe royale,
> Les regards attachés aux débris de sa tour,
> Il cria dans la nuit:—Tu mourras à ton tour!
> J'atteste par neuf fois les Runas immortelles,
> Tu mourras comme moi, Dieu des âmes nouvelles,
> Car l'homme survivra! Vingt siècles de douleurs
> Feront saigner sa chair et ruisseler ses pleurs,
> Jusqu'au jour où ton joug, subi deux mille années,
> Fatiguera le cou des races mutinées;
> Où les temples dressés parmi les nations
> Deviendront en risée aux générations;
> Et ce sera ton heure! et dans ton ciel mystique
> Tu rentreras, vêtu du suaire ascétique,
> Laissant l'homme futur, indifférent et vieux,
> Se coucher et dormir en blasphémant les Dieux!

7. Joseph Vianey, *op. cit.*, pp. 200–210.

8. *Les reptiles surpris rampent sous les épines;*
   L'orfraie et le hibou sortent en gémissant.

9. The concluding stanzas of "Le Barde de Temrah":

> Le vieux Barde, à ces mots, redressant sa stature,
> Prend l'épée, en son coeur il l'enfonce à deux mains
> Et tombe lentement contre la terre dure:
> —Ami, dis à ton Dieu que je rejouis les miens.—
>
> C'est ainsi que mourut, dit la sainte légende,
> Le chanteur de Temrah, Murdoc'h aux longs cheveux,
> Vouant au noir Esprit cette sanglante offrande.
>
> Le palais écroulé s'illumina de feux
> Livides, d'où sortit un grand cri d'épouvante.
> Le Barde avait rejoint les siens, selon ses voeux.
>
> Auprès du corps, dont l'âme, hélas! était vivante,
> L'Apôtre en gémissant courba les deux genoux;
> Mais Dieu n'exauça point son oraison fervente.

10. Joseph Vianey, *op. cit.*, pp. 88–89.

11. The concluding strophes of "Le Cœur de Hialmar":

> Viens par ici, Corbeau, mon brave mangeur d'hommes!
> Ouvre-moi la poitrine avec ton bec de fer.

Tu nous retrouveras demain tels que nous sommes.
Porte mon coeur tout chaud à la fille d'Ylmer.

Dans Upsal, où les Jarls boivent la bonne bière
Et chantent, en heurtant les cruches d'or, en chœur,
A trie-d'aile vole, ô rodeur de bruyère!
Cherche ma fiancée et porte-lui mon cœur.

12. From "Qaïn":

> *Eden! O Vision éblouissante et brève,*
> *Toi dont, avant les temps, j'étais déshérité!*
> *Eden, Eden! voici que mon cœur irrité*
> *Voit changer brusquement la forme de son rêve,*
> *Et le glaive flamboie à l'horizon quitté.*
>
> *Eden! ô le plus cher et le plus doux des songes,*
> *Toi vers qui j'ai poussé d'inutiles sanglots!*
> *Loin de tes murs sacrés éternellement clos*
> *La malédiction balaye, et tu plonges*
> *Comme un soleil perdu sans l'abîme des flots.*

13. From "Qaïn":

> *Je resterai debout! Et du soir à l'aurore,*
> *Et de l'aube à la nuit, jamais je ne tairai*
> *L'infatigable cri d'un cœur désespéré!*
> *La soif de la justice, ô Khéroub, me dévore.*
> *Ecrase-moi, sinon, jamais je ne ploîrai!*
>
> *Ténèbres, répondez! Qu'Iahvèh me réponde!*
> *Je souffre, qu'ai-je fait? Le Khéroub dit:—Qaïn!*
> *Iahvèh l'a voulu. Tais-toi. Fais ton chemin*
> *Terrible.—Sombre Esprit, le mal est dans le monde.*
> *Oh! pourquoi suis-je né?—Tu le sauras demain.—*
>
> *Je l'ai su. Comme l'ours aveuglé qui trébuche*
> *Dans la fosse où la mort l'a longtemps attendu,*
> *Flagellé de fureur, ivre, sourd, éperdu,*
> *J'ai heurté d'Iahvèh l'inévitable embûche;*
> *Il m'a précipité dans le crime tendu.*

14. Irving Putter, *op. cit.*, p. 320.

15. Charles Baudelaire, "Leconte de Lisle" in *L'Art romantique* (Paris: Garnier, 1962), p. 781.

16. Gaston Bachelard reproaches Leconte de Lisle for the application of an identical diagnosis to men and to animals. See his *Lautréamont* (Paris: Corti, 1939), pp. 161–62.

17. Joseph Vianey, *op. cit.*, p. 32.

18. The last strophe of "Les Hurleurs":
    Je ne sais; mais, ô chiens qui hurliez sur les plages,
    Après tant de soleils qui ne reviendront plus,
    J'entends toujours, du fond de mon passé confus
    Le cri désespéré de vos douleurs sauvages!

19. The concluding lines of "Le Rêve du jaguar":
    En un creux du bois sombre, interdit au soleil
    Il s'affaisse, allongé sur quelque roche plate;
    D'un large coup de langue il se lustre la patte;
    Il cligne ses yeux d'or hébétés de sommeil;
    Et, dans l'illusion de ses forces inertes,
    Faisant mouvoir sa queue et frissonner ses flancs,
    Il rêve qu'au milieu des plantations vertes,
    Il enfonce d'un bond ses ongles ruisselants
    Dans la chair des taureaux effarés et beuglants.

20. From "Le Sommeil du condor":
    Lui, comme un spectre, seul, au front du pic altier,
    Baigné d'une lueur qui saigne sur la neige,
    Il attend cette mer sinistre qui l'assiège:
    Elle arrive, déferle, et le couvre en entier.
    Dans l'abîme sans fond la Croix australe allume
    Sur les côtes du ciel son phare constellé.
    Il râle de plaisir, il agite sa plume,
    Il érige son cou musculeux et pelé,
    Il s'enlève en fouettant l'âpre neige des Andes,
    Dans un cri rauque il monte où n'atteint pas le vent,
    Et loin du globe noir, loin de l'astre vivant,
    Il dort dans l'air glacé, les ailes toutes grandes.

21. From "Les Eléphants":
    Ils rêvent en marchant du pays délaissé,
    Des forêts de figuiers où s'abrita leur race.
    Ils reverront le fleuve échappé des grands monts,
    Où nage en mugissant l'hippopotame énorme,
    Où, blanchis par la lune et projetant leur forme,
    Ils descendaient pour boire en écrasant les joncs.

22. From "La Vipère":
    Mais si l'amer venin est entré dans tes veines,
    Pâle de volupté pleurée et de langueur,
    Tu chercheras en vain un remède à tes peiness
    L'angoisse du néant te remplira le cœur.
    Ployé sous son fardeau de honte et de misère,
    D'un exécrable mal ne vis pas consumé:
    Arrache de ton sein la mortelle vipère,
    Ou tais-toi, lâche, et meurs, meurs d'avoir trop aimé!

23. The concluding strophes of "Christine":

Voici les pins noirs du vieux cimetière.
—Adieu, quitte-moi, reprends ton chemin;
Mon unique amour, entends ma prière!—
Mais Elle au tombeau descend la première,
Et lui tend la main.

Et, depuis ce jour, sous la croix de cuivre,
Dans la même tombe ils dorment tous deux.
O sommeil divin dont le charme enivre!
Ils aiment toujours. Heureux qui peut vivre
Et mourir comme eux!

24. Joseph Vianey, *op. cit.*, p. 59.

25. The closing strophes of "Le Manchy":

Tandis qu'un papillon, les deux ailes en fleur,
Teinte d'azur et d'écarlate,
Se posait par instants sur ta peau délicate
En y laissant de sa couleur.

On voyait au travers du rideau de batiste,
Tes boucles dorer e'oreiller
Et sous leurs cils mi-clos, feignant de sommeiller,
Tes beaux yeaux de sombre améthyste.

Tu t'en venais ainsi, par ces matins si doux,
De la montagne à la grand' messe,
Dans ta grâce naïve et ta rose jeunesse,
Au pas rythmé de tes Hinous.

Maintenant, dans le sable aride de nos grèves,
Sous les chiendents, au bruit des mers,
Tu reposes parmi les morts qui me sont chers,
O charme de mes premiers rêves!

26. From "La Fontaine aux lianes":

Au fond des bois baignés d'une vapeur céleste,
Il était une eau vive où rien ne rémuait;
Quelques joncs verts, gardiens de la forêt agreste
S'y penchaient au hasard en un groupe muet.

Les larges nénuphars, les lianes errantes,
Blancs archipels, flottaient enlacés sur les eaux,
Et dans leurs profondeurs vives et transparentes
Brillait un autre ciel où nageaient les oiseaux.

27. The concluding lines of "La Vérandah":

Tout se tait. L'oiseau grêle et le frelon jaloux
Ne se querellent plus autour des figures mûres

Les rosiers de l'Iran ont cessé leurs murmures,
Et l'eau vive s'endort dans les porphyres roux.

28. From "Ultra Coelos":

Mais, ô Nature, hélas! ce n'est point toi qu'on aime;
Tu ne fais point couler nos pleurs et notre sang,
Tu n'entends point nos cris d'amour ou d'anathème,
Tu ne recules point en nous éblouissant!

Ta coupe toujours pleine est trop près de nos lèvres;
C'est le calice amer du désir qu'il nous faut!
C'est le clairon fatal qui sonne dans nos fièvres:
Debout! Marchez, courez, volez, plus loin, plus haut!

29. From "La Vision de Snorr":

Enfin, je vois le Peuple antique, aveugle et fou,
La race qui vécut avant votre lumière,
Seigneur! et qui marchait, hélas! sans savoir où.

Tels qu'un long tourbillon de vivante poussière,
Le même vent d'erreur, les remue au hasard.
Et le soleil du Diable éblouit leur paupière.

Or, vous nous avez fait, certes, la bonne part,
A nous qui gémissons sur cette terre inique;
Mais pour les ancens morts vous êtes venu tard!

30. *Discours de réception à l'Académie Française prononcé le 31 mars 1887.*

31. The closing stanzas of "Un Acte de charité":

Aux angles du réduit de sapin et de chaume,
Versant des pleurs amers, elle alluma du feu:
J'ai fait ce que j'ai pu, je vous remets à Dieu,
Cria-t-elle, et Jésus vous ouvre son royaume!—

Tous passèrent ainsi dans leur éternité;
Prompte mort, d'une paix bienheureuse suivie.
Pour la Dame, en un cloître elle acheva sa vie.
Que Dieu la juge en son infallible équité!

32. Anatole France, *La Vie littéraire* I (Paris: Calmann-Lévy, 1889), 96–97.

33. From "Le Nazaréen":

Tu n'avais pas menti! Ton Eglise et ta gloire
Peuvent, ô Rédempteur, sombrer aux flots mouvants;
L'homme peut sans frémir rejeter ta mémoire,
Comme on livre un cendre inerte aux quatre vents;

Tu peux, sur les débris des saintes cathédrales,
Entendre et voir, livide et le front ceint de fleurs,

Se ruer le troupeau des folles saturnales,
Et son rire insulter tes divines douleurs!

34. From "L'Anathème":
Sinon, terre épuisée, où ne germe plus rien
Qui puisse alimenter l'espérance infinie,
Meurs! Ne prolonge pas ta muette agonie,
Rentre pour y dormir au flot diluvien.

35. From "Les Montreurs":
Dans mon orgueil muet, dans ma tombe sans gloire,
Dussé-je m'engloutir pour l'éternité noire,
Je ne te vendrai pas mon ivresse ou mon mal.

Je ne livrerai pas ma vie à tes huées,
Je ne danserai pas sur ton tréteau banal
Avec tes histrions et tes prostitués.

36. From "Aux Modernes":
Vous vivez lâchement, sans rêve, sans dessein,
Plus vieux, plus décrépits que la terre inféconde,
Châtrés dès le berceau par le siècle assassin
De toute passion vigoureuse et profonde.

Votre cervelle est vide autant que votre sein,
Et vous avez souillé ce misérable monde
D'un sang si corrompu, d'un souffle si malsain,
Que la mort germe seule en cette boue immonde.

37. Irving Putter, op. cit., p. 326.

38. From "Solvet seclum":
Ce sera quand le Globe et tout ce qui l'habite,
Bloc stérile arraché de son immense orbite,
Stupide, aveugle, plein d'un dernier hurlement,
Plus lourd, plus éperdu de moment en moment.
Contre quelque univers immobile en sa force
Défoncera sa vieille et misérable écorce.

Chapter Five

1. The concluding verses of "Les Siècles maudits":
L'écume de la rage aux dents, la torche en main,
Soufflant dans toute chair, dans toute âme vivante
L'angoisse d'être au monde autant que l'épouvante
De la mort, voue au feu stupide de l'enfer
L'holocauste fumant sur ton autel de fer!
Dans chacune de vos exécrables minutes
O siècles d'égorgeurs, de lâches et de brutes,

> *Honte de ce vieux globe et de l'humanité,*
> *Maudits, soyez maudits, et pour l'éternité!*

2. Irving Putter, *The Pessimism of Leconte de Lisle: The Work and the Time*, p. 187.

3. From "La Bête écarlate":

> *Et l'Homme s'éveille de son rêve, muet,*
> *Haletant et livide. Et tout son corps suait,*
> *D'angoisse et de dégoût devant cette géhenne*
> *Effroyable, ces flots de sang et cette haine,*
> *Ces siècles de douleurs, ces peuples abêtis,*
> *Et ce Monstre écarlate, et ces démons sortis*
> *Des gueules dont chacune en rugissant le nomme,*
> *Et cette éternité de tortures! Et l'Homme,*
> *S'abattant contre terre avec un grand soupir,*
> *Désepéra du monde, et désira mourir.*

4. From the second part of "Le Lévrier de Magnus":

> *Qu'il jouisse de tout ce qu'on rêve ici-bas,*
> *Richesse en plein soleil et volupté dans l'ombre,*
> *Et que Mahon l'accueille en ses joyeux sabbats!*

> *Il est brave, il est jeune et fort. Qui sait le nombre*
> *De ses jours triomphants? Son désir satisfait,*
> *Il se repentira quand viendra l'âge sombre.*

5. From the fourth part of "Le Lévrier de Magnus":

> *Magnus! Magnus! le Feu décorateur est prêt:*
> *L'Opale coule autour de ton doigt qu'elle enflamme.*
> *Oh! Répens-toi. Préviens l'irrévocable Arrêt.—*

> *Non! dit Magnus. Pourquoi Dieu m'a-t-il forgé l'âme*
> *De façon qu'elle rompe et ne puisse ployer?*
> *Ruisqu 'il l'a faite ainsi, qu'il en pirte le blâme!—*

6. From "L'Holocauste":

> *Et la foule y tournoie et s'y heurte et s'y rue*
> *Pêle-mêle, les yeux écarquillés, les bras*
> *En l'air: moines blancs, gris ou bruns, barbus ou ras,*
> *Chaux ou déchaux, ayant capes, frocs ou cagoules,*
> *Vieilles femmes grinçant des dents comme des goules,*
> *Cavaliers de sang noble, empanachés, pattus,*
> *Rogues, caracolant sur les pavés pointus,*
> *Dames à jupe roide en carrosses et chaises,*
> *Estafiers et soudards, et le confus troupeau*
> *Des manants et des gueux et des prostituées.*

7. See Edmond Eggli, ed., *Leconte de Lisle: poèmes choisis* (Manchaster, England: At the University Press, 1959), p. 130.

8. From "La Tête de Kenwarc'h":

Je ne l'entendrai plus, cette tête héroïque,
Sous le torque d'or roux commander et crier;
Mais je la planterai sur le fer de ma pique:
Elle ira devant moi dans l'ouragan guerrier.
Oc'h! Oc'h! C'est le Saxon qui l'entendera crier!

Elle me mènera, Kenwarc'h! jusqu'au lâche
Qui t'a troué le dos sur le Cap de Penn'hor.
Je lui romprai le cou du marteau de ma hache
Et je lui mangerai le cœur tout vif encor!

9. The last strophes of "Sacra fames":

Va! monstre! tu n'es pas autre que nous ne sommes,
Plus hideux, plus féroce, ou plus désespéré.
Console-toi! demain tu mangeras des hommes.
Demain par l'homme aussi tu seras dévoré.

La Faim sacrée est un long meurtre légitime
Des profondeurs de l'ombre aux cieux resplendissants,
Et l'homme et le requin, égorgeur ou victime,
Devant ta face, ô Mort, sont tous deux innocents.

10. The conclusion of "L'Albatros":

Seul, le Roi de l'espace et des mers sans rivages
Vole contre l'assaut des rafales sauvages.

D'un trait puissant et sûr, sans hâte ni retard,
L'œil dardé par delà le livide brouillard,
De ses ailes de fer rigidement tendues,
Il fend le tourbillon des rauques étendues,
Et, tranquille au milieu de l'épouvantement,
Vient, passe et disparaît majestueusement.

11. From "L'Incantation du loup":

L'Homme, le massacreur antique des aïeux,
De ses enfants et de la royale femelle
Qui leur versait le lait ardent de sa mamelle,
Hante immuablement son rêve furieux.

Une braise rougit sa prunelle énergique;
Et, redressant ses poils roides comme des clous,
Il évoque, en hurlant, l'âme des anciens loups
Qui dorment dans la lune éclatante et magique.

12. Baudelaire's "Harmonies du *soir*" in the *Fleurs du Mal* is a variation of the Malayan pantoum.

13. From "Pantoum malais I":

L'éclair vibre sa flèche torse
A l'horizon mouvant des flots.

> Sur ta natte de fine écorce
> Tu rêves, les yeux demi-clos.
>
> A l'horizon mouvant des flots
> La foudre luit sur les écumes.
> Tu rêves, les yeux demi-clos,
> Dans la case que tu parfumes.

14. From "Villanelle":

> Le Temps, l'Etendue et le Nombre
> Sont tombés du noir firmament
> Dans la mer immobile et sombre.
>
> Suaire de silence et d'ombre,
> La nuit efface absolument
> Le Temps, l'Etendue et le Nombre.

15. From "Le Frais Matin dorait":

> La Vierge aux pales mains t'a prise la première,
> Chère âme! Et j'ai vécu loin des gérofliers,
> Loin des sentiers charmants à tes pas familiers,
> Et loin du ciel natal où fleurit ta lumière.
>
> Des siècles ont passé, dans l'ombre ou la lumière,
> Et je revois toujours mes astres familiers,
> Les beaux yeux qu'autrefois, sous nos gérofliers,
> Les frais matin dorait de sa clarté première.

16. From "A Un Poète mort":

> Moi, je t'envie, au fond du tombeau calme et noir,
> D'être affranchi de vivre et de ne plus savoir
> La honte de penser et l'horreur d'être un homme.

17. From "L'Illusion suprême":

> Soit! la poussière humaine, en proie au temps rapide,
> Ses voluptés, ses pleurs, ses combats, ses remords,
> Les Dieux qu'elle a conçus et l'univers stupide
> Ne valent pas la paix impassible des morts.

18. From "La Maya":

> Eclair, rêve sinistre, éternité qui ment,,
> La vie antique est faite inépuisablement
> Du tourbillon sans fin des apparences vaines.

19. Fernand Desonay, *Le Rêve hellénique chez les poètes parnassiens*, p. 280.

20. Part I, Scene 3 of the *Erinnyes*:

> Sur les temples massifs, sur les palais ardents
> Que l'incendie avec mille langues hérisse,
> J'entends tourbilloner Pallas dévastatrice,
> Et la foule mugir et choir par grands morceaux,

Et les mères hurler d'horreur, quand les berceaux,
Du haut des toits fumants écrasés sur les pierres,
Trempent d'un sang plus frais les sandales guerrières.
Ah! la victoire est douce, et la vengeance aussi!
21. Part II, Scene 3 of the *Erinnyes:*
  Puisque l'heure est venue, il convient d'être prompt;
  La soif du sang me brûle, et le Destin m'entraîne.
  Femmes, qu'une de vous se hâte vers la Reine,
  Et dise: "Un voyageur qui nous est inconnu,
  O fille de Léda, dans Argos est venu.
  Il annonce.—que Zeus fasse mentir sa bouche!—
  Qu'Orestès est couché sur la funèbre couche."
  Elle viendra joyeuse!

Chapter Six

1. Jules Huret, *Enquête sur l'évolution littéraire* (Paris: Charpentier, 1891), pp. 310–11.
2. The concluding stanzas from "Les Raisons du Saint-Père":
  O Christ! Et c'est ainsi que, réformant ton rêve,
  Connaissant mieux que toi la vile humanité,
  Nous avons pris la pourpre et les Clefts et le Glaive,
  Et nous t'avons donné le monde épouvanté.

  Mais, arrivés d'hier à ce glorieux faîte,
  Il reste à supprimer l'hérétique pervers.
  Ne viens donc pas troubler l'œuvre bientôt parfaite
  Et rompre le filet jeté sur l'univers.

  Dans le sang de l'impie, au bruit des saints cantiques,
  Laisse agir notre Foi, ne nous interromps plus;
  Retourne et règne en paix dans les hauts cieux mystiques.
  Jusqu'à l'épuisement des siècles révolus.

  Car, aussi bien, un jour, dussions-nous disparaître,
  Submergés par les flots d'un monde soulevé,
  Grâce à nous, pour jamais, tu resteras, ô maître,
  Un Dieu, le dernier Dieu que l'homme aura rêvé.—

  Le Saint-Père se tut, prit sa croix pectorale
  Qu'il baisa par trois fois avec recueillement,
  * Et ce monde sans cause et sans terme où je passe*
  De ce qui fut le Christ s'effaça lentement.
3. From "La Paix des dieux":
  Vois! Mon âme est semblable à quelque morne espace

> *Où, seul, je m'interroge, où je me réponds seul,*
> *Et ce monde sans cause et sans terms où je passe*
> *M'enveloppe et m'étreint comme un lourd linceul.*

4. From "La Paix des dieux":

> *Vous en qui j'avais mis l'espérance féconde,*
> *Contre qui je luttais, fier de ma liberté,*
> *Si vous êtes tous morts, qu'ai-je à faire en ce monde,*
> *Moi, le premier croyant et le vieux révolté?—*
>
> *Et l'Homme crut entendre alors dans son être*
> *Une Voix qui disait, triste comme un sanglot:*
> *—Rien de tel, jamais plus, ne doit revivre ou naître;*
> *Les Temps balayeront tout cela flot sur flot.*

5. The concluding strophes of "L'Aigu Bruissement":

> *Tout n'était que lumière, amour, joie, harmonie;*
> *Et moi, bien qu'ébloui de ce monde charmant,*
> *J'avais au fond du cœur comme un gémissement,*
> *Un douloureux soupir, une plainte infinie,*
> *Très lointaine et très vague et triste amèrement.*
> *C'est que devant ta grâce et ta beauté, Nature!*
> *Enfant qui n'avais rien souffert ni deviné,*
> *Je sentais croître en moi l'homme prédestiné,*
> *Et je pleurais, saisi de l'angoisse future,*
> *Epouvanté de vivre, hélas! et d'être né.*

6. "Dans l'Air léger":

> *Dans l'air léger, dans l'azur rose,*
> *Un grêle fil d'or rampe et luit*
> *Sur les mornes que l'aube arrose.*
>
> *Fleur ailée, au matin éclose,*
> *L'oiseau s'éveille, vole et fuit*
> *Dans l'air léger, dans l'azur rose.*
>
> *L'abeille boit ton âme, ô rose!*
> *L'épais tamarinier bruit*
> *Sous les mornes que l'aube arrose.*
>
> *Et la mer, où le ciel repose,*
> *Fait monter son vaste et doux bruit*
> *Sur les mornes que l'aube arrose.*
>
> *Mais les yeux divins que j'aimais*
> *Se sont fermés, et pour jamais,*
> *Dans l'air léger, dans l'azur rose!*

7. Joseph Vianey, *Les Sources de Leconte de Lisle*, pp. 304–5.

8. From "Toi par qui j'ait senti":

> *Toi par qui jai senti, pour des heures trop brèves,*
> *Ma jeunesse renaître et mon coeur refleurir,*
> *Sois bénie à jamais! J'aime, je puis mourir;*
> *J'ai vécu le meilleur et le plus beau des rêves!*

9. Part I, Scene II of *L'Apollonide*:

> *O sources, qui jamais ne serez épuisées,*
> *Qui fluez et chantez harmonieusement*
> *Dans les mousses, parmi les lys lourds de rosées,*
> *A la pente du mont solitaire et charmant!*
> *Eaux vives! sur le seuil et les marches Pythiques*
> *Epanchez le trésor de vos urnes d' azur,*
> *Et puisse aussi le flot de mes jours fatidiques*
> > *Couler comme vous, chaste et pur!*
> *Mais une ombre soudaine et de confus murmures*
> *Viennent des pics neigeux et sortent des ramures.*
> *Ils passent au ciel clair sur le Temple et les bois.*
> *C'est le vol matinal des oiseaux. Je les vois!*

10. Part II, Scene IV of *L'Apollonide*:

> *O bel Archer, tes légers traits,*
> *Sous le feuillage des forêts*
> *Qui frémit, que le matin dore,*
> *Ne suivront plus dans l'air sonore*
> *Le vol des sauvages ramiers;*
> *Et jamais plus, dans les halliers*
> *Que parfume l'odeur des sèves,*
> *Nous ne charmerons tes doux rêves!*

11. Part I, Scene VIII of *L'Apollonide*:

> *Il germe ici plus beau, verdoyant dans l'aurore!*
> *Aussi doux qu'une lyre il chante au vent sonore,*
> *Et la Muse divine, avec ses belles mains,*
> *Ne le pose jamais sur des fronts inhumains.*

12. Part III, Scene VII of *L'Apollonide*:

> *Nous sommes les Vierges sacrées,*
> *Délices du vaste univers,*
> *Aux mitres d'or, aux lauriers verts,*
> *Aux lèvres toujours inspirées.*
> *L'homme éphémère et soucieux*
> *Et l'Ouranide au fond des cieux*
> *Sont illuminés de nos flammes,*
> *Et, parfois, nous réjouissons*
> *De nos immortelles chansons*
> *Le noir Hadès où sont les âmes.*

Selected Bibliography

PRIMARY SOURCES

1. Editions of Leconte de Lisle's Works

Leconte de Lisle, *Poésies complètes*. 4 volumes. The definitive text with notes and variants. Paris: Alphonse Lemerre, 1927.

Leconte de Lisle, *Premières poèsies et lettres intimes*. Edited by B. Guinaudeau. Paris: Fasquelle, 1902.

La Dernière Illusion de Leconte de Lisle: lettres inédites à Emilie Leforestier. Edited with critical notes, appendices, and a valuable introductory essay by Irving Putter. Berkeley and Los Angeles: University of California Press, 1968.

Leconte de Lisle: articles, préfaces, discours. Edited with notes and an introductory essay by Edgard Pich. Paris: Société d'Edition "Les Belles Lettres," 1971.

2. Anthologies

Leconte de Lisle: poèmes choisis. Edited with notes and an introductory essay by Edmond Eggli. Manchester, England: At the University Press, 1959.

Choix de poèmes de Leconte de Lisle. With notes and an essay by Pierre Gallissaires. Paris: Librairie Larousse "Classiques Larousse," 1969.

Leconte de Lisle in *Twelve French Poets: 1820–1901*. With an introduction and notes by Douglas Parmée. New York: David McKay Company ,1962.

Leconte de Lisle in *French Lyrics of the Nineteenth Century*, pp. 218–56. With introduction and notes by George N. Henning. Boston: Ginn and Co., 1913.

Leconte de Lisle in *French Poetry of the Nineteenth Century*. Second Edition. Selected and edited with introductions and critical notes by Elliott M. Grant. New York: The Macmillan Company, 1962.

SECONDARY SOURCES

BRERETON, GEOFFREY. *An Introduction to the French Poets*. New York: Barnes and Noble, 1960. Chapter 14 is a good general introduction to Leconte de Lisle.

CANAT, RENÉ. *Du Sentiment de la solitude morale chez les Romantiques et les Parnassiens*. Geneva: Slatkine Reprints, 1967. Chapter 9 is an illuminating discussion of the manner of the Parnassians in general and of Leconte de Lisle in particular.

CASSAGNE, ALBERT. *La Théorie de l'art pour l'art en France chez les derniers romantiques et les premiers réalistes.* Paris: Lucien Dorbon, 1959. Probably the best single study available on Art for Art's Sake and Parnassianism. Under Part Two, Chapters 4, 5, and 6 provide stimulating analyses of Parnassian objectivity, pessimism, and plasticity.

CHADBOURNE, RICHARD. "The Generation of 1848: Four Writers and their Affinities," *Essays in French Literature* V (1968): 1–21. A penetrating discussion of the literary interrelationships between Leconte de Lisle, Baudelaire, Flaubert, and Renan.

DESONAY, FERNAND. *Le Rêve hellénique chez les poètes parnassiens.* Paris: Honoré Champion, 1928. A valid analysis of the types of Hellenism espoused by Louis Ménard and Leconte de Lisle.

FAIRLIE, ALISON. *Leconte de Lisle's Poems on the Barbarian Races.* Cambridge, England: At the University Press, 1947. An eminently useful study of Leconte de Lisle's sources for the *Poèmes barbares.*

FALSHAW, GLADYS. *Leconte de Lisle et l'Inde.* Paris: d'Arthez, 1923. Still a generally informative treatise on Leconte de Lisle's Hinduism.

FLOTTES, PIERRE. *Leconte de Lisle: l'homme et l'œuvre.* Paris: Hatier-Boivin, 1954. A lucid presentation of the life and work of Leconte de Lisle with a decided emphasis on psycho-analytical techniques.

GRANT, ELLIOTT. *French Poetry and Modern Industry: 1830–1870.* Cambridge, Mass.: Harvard University Press, 1927. A valuable documentary study of the influences of industry upon literature in general and poetry in particular. The sections devoted to Maxime Du Camp, Louis Bouihlet, and Leconte de Lisle go a long way in explaining the latter's antipragmatic attitude.

KRAMER, CORNELIS. *André Chénier et la poésie parnassienne.* Paris: Honoré Champion, 1925. The chief value of this thesis rests upon the author's general sketch of the state of lyricism during the so-called Parnassian period. Kramer asserts rather than illustrates the links that he establishes between Chénier and Leconte de Lisle.

MARTINO, PIERRE. *Parnasse et Symbolisme.* Paris: Armand Colin, 1925. Chapters 3 through 6 discuss in a general way Leconte de Lisle's role in the Parnassian movement.

PEYRE, HENRI. *Louis Ménard.* New Haven: Yale University Press, 1932. Chapter 8, "Louis Ménard et le Parnasse," is a perceptive analysis of the interrelationships which existed between Ménard and de Lisle.

Selected Bibliography

PRIOU, JULES-MARIE. *Leconte de Lisle*. Paris: Pierre Seghers, 1966. This anthology of de Lisle's major verse is complemented by a good analysis of the life and the work of the poet.

PUTTER, IRVING. *Leconte de Lisle and His Contemporaries*. Berkeley: University of California Press, 1951. A very carefully researched and clearly presented study of critical reaction to Leconte de Lisle during his own lifetime and in the twentieth century.

————. *The Pessimism of Leconte de Lisle: Sources and Evolution.* Berkeley: University of California Press, 1954.

————. *The Pessimism of Leconte de Lisle: The Work and The Time.* University of California Press, 1961. These two volumes constitute the most comprehensive study on de Lisle and his art as a poet. Emphasis is placed on the philosophical implications of the poet's position as an artist. Putter considers the poems in separate rubrics, such as: "the lyrical desire," "youth and the past," "love," "the problem of evil," "the Hindu approach: suffering," etc. A rewarding study from every viewpoint.

SOURIAU, MAURICE. *Histoire du Parnasse*. Paris: 1929. Somewhat dated, chatty approach to the Parnassians and Leconte de Lisle. A good overview of the entire situation results nevertheless.

VIANEY, JOSEPH. *Les Sources de Leconte de Lisle*. Montpellier: Coulet, 1907. A generally valid study of the sources of the poet's major verse.

————. *Les Poèmes barbares de Leconte de Lisle*. Paris: Malfère, 1933. Good background material for the major poems which constitute de Lisle's second major collection.

Index

Index